HANK WILLIAMS
SNAPSHOTS FROM THE LOST HIGHWAY

COLIN ESCOTT & KIRA FLORITA

FOREWORD BY RICK BRAGG   PREFACE BY MARTY STUART

HANK WILLIAMS

SNAPSHOTS FROM THE LOST HIGHWAY

★ ★ ★ ★ ★ ★ ★ ★ ★

DA CAPO PRESS

Design by Cooley Design Lab, NYC

Cataloging-in-Publication data for this book is available from the Library of Congress.

First Da Capo Press edition 2001

ISBN: 0-306-81052-2

Published by **DA CAPO PRESS**
A Member of the Perseus Books Group
www.dacapopress.com

Da Capo Press books are available at special discounts for bulk purchases in the U.S. by corporations, institutions, and other organizations. For more information, please contact the Special Markets Department at the Perseus Books Group, Eleven Cambridge Center, Cambridge, Massachusetts 02142, or call 617-252-5298.

1 2 3 4 5 6 7 8 9 — 05 04 03 02 01

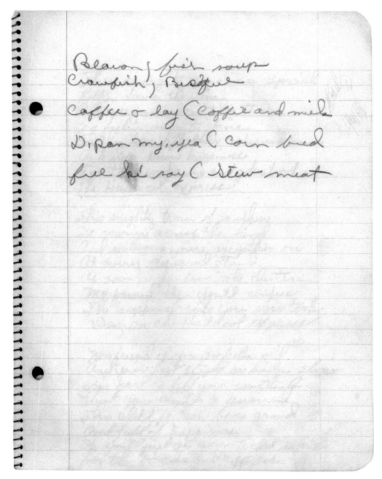

Hank researches the ingredients of "Jambalaya."

CONTENTS

ACKNOWLEDGMENTS

Almost inevitably, we're going to overlook some of the people who helped us with this book. During the three years between inception and publication, almost everyone involved underwent career or personal changes, so the work was often done at unsociable hours. We owe our biggest vote of thanks to Marty Stuart, Acuff-Rose Music, Hank Williams, Jr., and Jett Williams for opening their archives to us. Without them, of course, the book would not have been feasible. We'd especially like to thank Maria-Elena Orbea at Marty's office, Peggy Lamb and Jerry Bradley at Acuff-Rose, Merle Kilgore and Linda Woodard at Hank Jr's office, and Jett's husband and business partner, Keith Adkinson. Our agent, Amy Williams, took our book around to the few believers in New York. Fortunately, Andrea Schulz at the Da Capo Press division of Perseus Books saw what we saw, and worked unstintingly to make it happen. Thanks also to Jane Snyder and Kevin Hanover at Da Capo. For support and advice, we're grateful to David Gernert of The Gernert Company; Luke Lewis, Chairman of Mercury Nashville and President of Lost Highway Records; Tammy Young at AdJett Productions; and to Peter Guralnick, Ernst Jorgensen, Cal Morgan, Rick Bragg, and designer Steven Cooley.

Among the fans who made materials available to us, we owe a special debt of gratitude to David Mitchell, Bill Whatley, and George Merritt. Additionally, David Dennard, Jurgen Koop, Donald Daily, Glenn Sutton, and Pete Howard gave us previously unpublished images. Former Drifting Cowboy Don Helms, now sadly one of the few surviving members of Hank's bands, helped identify photos, as did Hank's cousin, Walter McNeil, and Red Foley's former steel guitarist, Billy Robinson. And, finally, we'd like to acknowledge the late Dorothy Horstman, who made her Audrey Williams interview available to us.

Thanks also to those around us, especially Pat, Marrah, and Ricky, who heard more about Hank Williams than they ever wanted to know. Now we're back.

Colin Escott and Kira Florita

FOREWORD BY RICK BRAGG

When he died on the way to a show on New Year's Day 1953, the Yankee newspapers called him a "hillbilly star."

He was declared dead in Oak Hill, West Virginia, but everyone knows he died in the back seat of a big sedan as it rushed along the blacktop, so there is no way to tell, really, where he died, on which mile of asphalt, in which zip code. How long did his spiritless body ride, before the car's driver shook him, to see if he was okay?

It's just one more little thing about him we will never know. We only know he was 29, which is not much life at all, and that he suffered from a back misery so intense that it left him bone white under the stage lights, and that he died in a car somewhere between a snowed-in airport in Knoxville and a coroner's inquest in Oak Hill, and that the greatest country music singer who ever was and probably ever will be passed into history.

A hillbilly star.

It might have been the fact he sang under a cowboy hat, or that he was from Alabama, or it might have been his spelling and pronunciation, that made them call him that. He spelled things the way they sounded, like hillbillies do, and punctuated them with sorrow, love and regret. Like this song, which he wrote for his wife Audrey after she left him.

> We met we lived and dear we loved
> Then came that fatal day
> The love that we felt so dear
> Fade far away
> To night we both are alone
> And heres all that I can say
> I love you still and all ways will
> But thats the price we have to pay

It was almost like the words poured straight out of his heart and bypassed his head, and for the people in the auditoriums that smelled of floor wax and popcorn, it was like they swirled from the microphone straight through their ears and down, down, deep into their own hearts. Heads didn't have much to do with it. Hillbillies are funny that way.

Now, almost a half-century later, he is brilliant, the music experts say. It's the same music, but the hillbilly star is now pure genius. He is a pioneer, an innovator. I guess there are just a lot more hillbillies now, in high places.

Some people like to go stand by his grave, but I never wanted to do that. That would be admitting that he is finished, that he is gone.

He is not. Hank Williams is merely dead, and that is not at all the same thing.

I am not like those Elvis fans—good people, a lot of them—who won't admit that the King is dead. I wonder, sometimes, if what they really see, when they see him at the Waffle House, the Wal-Mart or the Shriner's Pancake Breakfast, is their own heart. They wish him alive, so strongly.

It's not that way with me and Hank, with a lot of people and Hank. Hank is dead, his body is dust and bones, and he will never again walk up to a microphone, so thin and elegant in his Nashville-tailored Western suits, and sing his heart out. He is dead, free from the whiskey that wobbled him, free from the pain in his spine and soul, free from the demons that flogged him, free to sleep in ever-lasting peace—unless you believe in the heaven he sometimes sang about.

But gone?

Not as long as there is electricity, or dusty radios, or pawnshop guitars, or people who believe that music is a story, a story about people like them.

Like most people who sing something so true that it makes us cry, or at least makes us smile and tap our toes, he left tracks in the red dirt and black bottomland and Gulf Coast sand, and left pieces of himself in photos and scrawled-out song lyrics and faded posters of shows he performed and some he never showed up to at all. But people still don't know him, really. They have seen only specks and glimmers and slivers, maybe because his life was so short, but more likely because that is about all he lets us see. Even the very old, the ones who were alive when he sang his music at country fairs, who filled auditoriums in Montgomery and Bossier City, know little more than those of us who know his music from hearing our mommas sing his words over dish pans. And we, in turn, know only a little more than the ones who came after us, who heard his words for the first time on gleaming compact discs that have had the scratches magically lifted away.

So we are hungry for the details, for insights, maybe even for answers to why he was able to bend us the way he did, and why he did not last. We want to know little things as much as monumental things. I guess we just want to know, period.

Here, in these pages, Kira Florita and Colin Escott hand us some answers—and, if not answers, at least insights, evidence, sometimes even pieces of his heart. They raise a flap on the circus tent of his life, and let us sneak through, one fuzzy photograph and scrap of correspondence at a time. Why do we need it so, those of us who grew up with his music, and found it only in boxed sets? It has, I believe, everything to do with what is real in music, and what is not.

Smart people can talk about his impact on American music as a whole, and it seems like every day some guitar slinger with pink-tipped hair is saying how he feels some of his best words were influenced by Hank Williams, dude. I know he has been borrowed from just as he borrowed himself—from the bluegrass and the buck dancers and the white and black men who sang to their mules as they worked themselves half to death and sometimes all the way.

But there seems, to me, precious little of him that actually shines through in the music of the young, and that may very well be why those of us who love his music will never move on from it, and why he seems to find new fans every day among people who think music should be more than reverb and pierced belly buttons and pounding monotony.

Even among country musicians, he is as different as a rattlesnake is from a coiled garden hose. There seems no real country in it, except the hats. The women wear Versace, and sing about affairs in the summer before their boyfriend left for college. The men? All hat and no cow, most of them. One even sings about his girlfriend leaving him in a goddamned Suzuki.

I will never forget sitting in a music hall in St. Petersburg and listening as a man in a big hat, a warm-up act for Allison Krauss, took the stage and sang cliches. And then—I am not making this up—he referred to himself as moi.

Moi.

College.

Suzuki.

I guess some people would say it is country for the new world, the new age, but it is not country at all—it is pop music in snap pearl buttons, and it should be more than that.

It should be Hank—or at least Merle or Johnny Horton or Johnny Cash or Patsy Cline or George Jones or, more lately, Steve Earle. But much of what is good, today and forever, you can see Hank in it. We have to look back, all the way back to Hank, because that is where the words and the music and the talent converge for more than just mere sound—forgettable sound.

His fans, now, range from Harvard professors to New York book editors to concrete finishers and laid-off cotton mill workers. College students study his language; dropout guitar pickers, somewhere at this very moment, are picking through "I Can't Help It (If I'm Still In Love With You)" or "Lost Highway," and singing it in accents that would have made Hank smile.

I guess we can share him with them. I have no claim on him, really. He was dead before I was born. His live voice belongs to my kin, who heard him on the radio, singing and selling tonic, who paid one dollar and twenty cents to hear him sing sacred songs and pretended not to like the other ones, but they did. He belongs to my grandmother, Ava, who sang him to me, and to my momma, and to every old drunk man who ever tried to tune a guitar on the front porches of my life.

Once, marooned by an ice storm in Atlanta with a tall, redheaded woman, I played her some Hank Williams. She was from Staten Island, and I did not think it would take.

Before the ice had melted, she was singing "I'm So Lonesome I Could Cry."

June 2001

PREFACE BY MARTY STUART

Gary Walker owns a vintage record store in Nashville, Tennessee. One day he called to ask me if the name Irene Williams Smith meant anything to me. When I said no, he said, "She heard the song you wrote about Hank Williams, 'Me & Hank & Jumping Jack Flash,' and wants to talk to you about it...she's Hank's sister." Gary had recently met Irene at an event in Texas honoring Lefty Frizell. Moved by the aura of history surrounding her and what she had to say about it, he urged me to call her. I did...and it was life changing. On that call, we talked about my song, the weather, her childhood, and her brother, whom she referred to as Hiram, his given name. As we were about to hang up I asked where she lived. When she told me that she lived in a suburb of Dallas, I told her about an upcoming concert I was going to be playing at Texas Stadium. I invited her to come and she accepted.

When the day of the concert arrived, I sent for her. Gary Walker had flown in from Nashville to join me, and after the show we offered to take her to dinner. She said she wanted a taco and asked if I knew of any Mexican restaurants with Chinese maître d's. When I said no, she laughed and said, "I do, and you need to meet this maître d', because he likes my brother's songs." Then she added, "It's a strange place...you might like it."

When we arrived at the restaurant, the maître d' asked Irene if I was a friend of hers. She replied, "He's a friend of my brother." It was a disarming statement, and I knew instantly that she was checking my heart, scanning my soul, and searching for any unfit motives. "My experience," she said after we were seated, "is that our family has been taken advantage of in every way imaginable. I don't trust this world or the things of it. I live in my own world, and I'm careful with whom I share my thoughts." I knew this wasn't a time for words. It was a matter of waiting on the truth to reveal itself. As Tom Petty so eloquently put it, "The waiting is the hardest part." I dreaded her truth. As a matter of fact, it scared the hell out of me. I didn't have anything to hide, but I sensed that Irene had something she was holding until she had made up her mind as to whether or not she could trust me with it.

As we ate in silence, I found myself on trial. I knew if she found me unsuitable I could simply pay the check, go to the hotel, and call it a day. It seemed to be the easiest way out, and I was beginning to favor it. However, I sensed that if she found what she was looking for in me, a door that had been locked for many years would be opened to me. It had a powerful presence around it. I couldn't tell if it was from Heaven or Hell. And I didn't know if I was ready for what was on the other side of it. I only knew I was caught up in it.

After a while, she finally broke her silence by asking, "Would you like to come to my house and see some of my brother's things?" "I think so," I said. So Gary and I took her to a Spanish neighborhood outside of Dallas where she lived in a small duplex. When we got out of the car, I heard a gunshot a couple of streets over. Without even looking up, she said, "Meet the neighbors." Walking to the porch of her duplex, I realized that the door I'd sensed in the restaurant was now right in front of me. It had steel bars on it just like the ones on her windows, and in front of it, hanging down from the porch ceiling, was a naked light bulb. I stopped for a moment and stared at it. I remember thinking that Hank's song "I Saw the Light" was about to take on a whole new meaning for me.

Once inside, Gary and I were invited to sit at her table. She walked over, took my hand, and said, "The things that I want to share with you are all I have left of my life with my family. You must understand that my brother is not Hank Williams—not to me. His name is Hiram; my mother's name is Lillian. I feel safe inviting you to our family dinner table. However, you must approach it with respect. Under those terms you are welcome."

For the next four or five hours she brought out hats, ties, suits, boxes, and albums of photographs, all of which the world had never seen. From time to time she would say, "I can't remember where I put it, but there's something I want you to hold." Then she would rifle through a pile of papers and say, "Oh, here it is," handing me objects like the manuscript of Hank's "Cold, Cold Heart" or a letter he sent to his mother from Handley, Texas. There was his birth certificate, his death certificate, and an identification badge from when he was employed at a southern Alabama shipyard. There was a letter from Dr. Toby Marshall begging Lillian's forgiveness in any part that he might have played in her son's death. ☞

There were letters from Fred Rose chastising Hank for always bumming money, drinking too much, and allowing Audrey's jealousies to drive him to destructive behavior. There were Hank's reading glasses from childhood, bits and pieces of unfinished songs, his tackle box full of fishing lures and pocket knives, two pairs of his boots, his report cards, stacks of legal documents from court entanglements after his death, his record collection, all of the cards sent to the family after his death, a picture of him and his first girlfriend, his first cowboy scarf, dice, a straight razor, and an ink pen. She handed me a phone message dated 12/30/52 from Dr. Marshall to Hank's mom that read, "Dr. Marshall would like to talk with the boy who is driving Hank." Then she handed me the telegram that she received from her mother about Hank's death. It read simply, "Come at once, Hank is dead."

She had two sets of pictures taken during the funeral and a recording of the service. I couldn't get over the image of the black family standing at the casket paying their respects. Taking place in a very racial South, this image spoke volumes to me about how deeply Hank Williams touched people. And finally, Irene showed me a handwritten card from a nun in Gulfport, Mississippi. It was addressed to Hank's mother and contained the message that Hank had recently delivered a donation to some orphaned children in her parish and while he was there had made it plain that he had settled up with his maker. Irene told me that her mother had been tormented after Hank's death by the thought that Hank had not made his peace with God. "This card," she said, "was heaven sent." With that, she closed her scrapbook and said, "I want you to help protect my brother's memory. When you hear people say bad things about him, take up for him." I really didn't know what that meant at that time; I understand it better now.

The trip back to the hotel is but a clouded memory now. I couldn't talk about that night for a long time. When I did, it was mostly with Gary Walker. I'm glad he had been there. It would be hard to explain some of the things we saw and felt that night without a witness.

I stayed in touch with Irene after that. One day she decided that she wanted to sell me a lot of Hank's things. She said she would make up her mind what she wanted to sell and how much it would cost. After she sent me a batch of things once, I asked her, "Why me?" She said, "You need the responsibility."

During the holidays that same year, I called to wish her a Merry Christmas. When I asked her if she had her shopping done, she laughed and said, "I don't have enough money to buy paper towels much less Christmas presents." So I sent her enough to live on for a year. She called and asked "Why me?" I said, "Just because." She said, "I think I will buy me a dress. It's been so long since I've had a new one."

The next time I saw Irene was to say goodbye. She was wearing her new dress and being laid to rest in a grave next to her brother Hiram. As the service was coming to an end, Bocephus stood in that red Alabama dirt and sang a bone-chilling a cappella version of "I Saw The Light" in those lonesome tones that God gave especially to him and his daddy. As he was singing I remembered Irene having said to me once, "I want to go home in the spring and see the dogwoods in bloom. I want to visit my family."

Irene wanted to share her memories. So many of them are included in this book. I invite you in and request that you approach what you are about to encounter with respect. Public property has feelings too.

June 2001

INTRODUCTION

Almost half-a-century has passed since Hank Williams last entered a recording studio, yet he's still among us. You'll have to go far to find someone who doesn't know "Jambalaya," "Your Cheatin' Heart," "I'm So Lonesome I Could Cry," "You Win Again," or "Cold, Cold Heart." Maybe they're not always known as Hank Williams songs, but they're known. Meanwhile, the world Hank walked has almost gone. In a few small Southern towns, you can still see or infer some of what he saw, but a little more disappears every year. Yet if you're an up-and-coming artist, now more than ever it's obligatory to cite him among your influences. His music has endured; alone among his contemporaries, Hank Williams reaches generations that neither knew him nor saw him.

A long and winding road brought us to this book. As an employee and a contractee of Mercury Records, we first worked on the restoration of Hank Williams's catalog. Hank recorded for MGM Records before its acquisition by Mercury/Polygram, but MGM had not always treated his recordings with respect. He'd been reinvented according to the season. When rock 'n' roll came along in the years after his death, MGM recorded over the fiddle and steel guitar parts with electric guitar and piano. During the Nashville Sound era, the original recordings were overdubbed once more, this time with strings. We took the view that Hank's music needed no more ornamentation than it had when he made it. Restored to its original form, it would be heard anew, we believed. Who could remain unmoved by its dignity, directness, and soulfulness? Hank Williams didn't overthink the making of music. His elements remained the most basic: a folksy melody; situations wrested from everyday life; an unfussy backing; and vocals delivered as if they were pages torn from a diary.

The same few photos had been used again and again on all the LPs and nearly everything published about Hank, so we tried hard to locate rare or unpublished shots for our record compilations. They were very well-received by the media and the public, perhaps because they came out at a time when Hank's music was being discovered by a new audience. Around 1996, it was decided that the time was right for a boxed set of his complete works. We realized the photos we had discovered when we were doing the compilations had only scratched the surface when our research for the boxed set uncovered a trove of previously unpublished photos and previously unreleased recordings. One afternoon, near the end of the research phase, we sat in the Mercury conference room and spread out all the photos, letters, and ephemera we'd found. Sequencing them in rough chronological order, we realized we were seeing more of Hank's life than had ever been seen before. In some photos, we saw the determination that drove him from the Alabama honky tonks to the top of his profession; in others, taken toward the end of his life, he looked unnaturally bloated and occasionally unkempt. So much happened in so few years. We knew the story well enough, but in those photos it seemed to come alive.

And soon we realized that there was even more material to be found. Marty Stuart had forged a relationship with Hank's sister, Irene, and had purchased her collection of photos and personal effects. It was still being sorted and catalogued when we finished the boxed set, which appeared in 1998 as *The Complete Hank Williams,* and it was only later that Marty showed us the full extent of what he had acquired. We also discovered that Hank's music publisher, Acuff-Rose, had books of unpublished songs in manuscript form. And when the Williams heirs, Hank Jr. and Jett, got the boxed set, they liked what they saw and promised access to their personal archives in the event that we did another project. Hank Jr. showed us the scrapbooks that his mother, Audrey, kept for his father; and Jett let us see what she had accumulated. We knew there would never be another comprehensive boxed set in which we could use all of this remarkable material, and so this book was born.

Most of the photos in this book are being published for the first time. We have tried to include as many as possible from the less-documented areas of Hank's life: youth, adolescence, performances, early days in and around Montgomery, and budding stardom in Shreveport. Some of the photos were dated and labeled with names and places; many others came without any identification at all—perhaps they were taken by fans, then sent to Hank, or sent later to his mother. Almost all of the photos were in no particular order, and it took some sleuthing to first group them, then figure out who accompanied Hank. Everything we've been able to discover is included in the captions. There are almost no color photographs from that time; those that still exist are actually color-tinted, or the color has faded away. We also chose a disproportionate number of photos from the funeral, both because so few of them had ever been seen and because it was an event that clearly moved many people. It cut across social and color barriers like no other to that point. Even back then, many who'd only heard Hank thought they knew him and roughly 25,000 of them felt compelled to attend. That's how direct and personal his music was. His family and close friends were at the funeral too, of course. They'd seen him go to the brink so often, never thinking that he'd fall. He was, after all, just twenty-nine.

Like the photographs, the song lyrics are truly special and almost entirely unpublished. Knowing what we know of Hank, who can fail to be moved by songs like "I Wish I Had a Dad"? There's a date on some of the lyrics, but most were undated. Placement, therefore, is not necessarily chronological. Some were written as neatly as Hank could write, ready for submission to Acuff-Rose; others were scrawled almost illegibly. (We have transcribed the lyrics as completely as possible in the Song Appendix, where you can go to see if your reading of Hank's writing matches ours.) Perhaps they were written in the backseat of a car, or after an argument; perhaps backstage in the dark, or after a few drinks. Hank wrote in a giddy, untutored scrawl, and his spelling was phonetic. Some of the lyrics—misspelled, crossed-through, crudely articulate—almost seem like a form of folk art.

Surrounded by all these artifacts, we felt that we finally came to know Hank Williams as well as anyone can in this twenty-first century. The responsibility for compiling and marketing his music has now passed to other hands, and this book concludes our day-to-day involvement. Here, we've let those who knew Hank tell the story. We feel that in their words and in these images, you too will come to know the man who shaped American music as few have.

Colin Escott and Kira Florita
Nashville, May 2001

1 "I WISH I HAD A DAD..."

The house no longer stands and the small settlement of Mount Olive West, Alabama, barely exists, but it was there, in a double-pen log house, that Hank Williams was born. His parents, Lon and Lillie Williams, married in 1916. Their first child, Irene, was born in 1922, and Hiram, later known as Hank, followed on September 17, 1923.

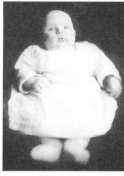

The only known infant photo of Hank

Lillie and Lon Williams, circa 1916

"If you will listen a song I will sing, about my daddy who ran a log train/Way down in the Southland in ol' Alabam, we lived in a place they call Chapman town" (from "The Log Train"). Several of Hank's relatives on both sides of his family worked for the lumber companies. Here, Hank, about age thirteen, joins his mother, Lillie, his sister, Irene, and his cousin J. C. McNeil in front of one of the W. T. Smith log trains.

"I chose [Hiram's] name from the Scripture, I Kings, 7TH Chapter, 13TH verse. I was born in Macedonia in Lowndes County, Alabama. I was a railroad engineer for a number of years. During the War I served with the 113TH Regiment of Engineers, Headquarters Detachment, in France. At the time of my boy's birth, I was farming strawberries in Butler County, and due to the late freeze lost what I had, and went back to railroad work to support my family. I bought a home a mile and a half from Georgiana and we lived there for two years. Working in logging camps, I was transferred from Chapman to the Ruthven job, and then bought a home in McWilliams in 1927, continuing with the Ruthven job until the summer of 1929. My health got worse due to service in the War….My health failing, I had to go to the Veterans Hospital. In January 1930, my son Hiram was taken to an uncle's home in Garland." *(Lon Williams, undated letter to* The Progressive Era, *Camden, Alabama)*

Lon was employed by the W. T. Smith Lumber Company until he stopped working in September 1929. Late in life, Hank wrote a ballad, "The Log Train," casting a rosy glow over what little he could remember of Lon's working years, but he saw his father rarely after Lon entered the Veterans Administration hospital in Alexandria, Louisiana. Family members say that Lon's face was paralyzed for several years, leading to a diagnosis of dementia. Contact between Lon and Lillie virtually ceased as Lillie faced the daunting task of raising her family alone during the Depression.

"When our dad went into the hospital, our uncle, Walter McNeil, moved us to Garland, Alabama, where we were with his family of five and our grandmother Skipper. Our mother woke us to hoe and pick cotton and strawberries. We lived there until mother was able to save enough to move to Georgiana, Alabama, where we stayed until the house we lived in burned. We left with the clothes we were sleeping in and our dad's shotgun, which Mother grabbed as we were going out the door. After the fire, we moved in again with the McNeils. People donated what they could. This was the Great Depression. Our mother worked as a practical nurse, cleaned houses, and hired herself out to kill, clean and dress hogs. She was superintendent of a canning factory. She kept boarders at rooming houses in Greenville and

Lillie's family, the Skippers, including her brother-in-law, Walter McNeil, who helped her out in the years after Lon left. First row, L-R; Hank, Ralph Skipper, Vollie Mae Skipper, Taft Skipper, Ollie Ray Skipper, J. C. McNeil, Opal McNeil, Irene Williams, Bernice McNeil, Marie McNeil. Second row; Lillie, Walter McNeil, Alice McNeil holding Walter McNeil Jr., Mrs. Ed Skipper, Ed Skipper holding Eddie Lee, Letch Skipper holding Bill, Zell Skipper, Mrs. John Skipper, Bob Skipper, and Grover McNeil

Montgomery. 'Any honest work to feed and clothe my children,' she used to say....She made our clothes from whatever was available (feed sacks, old clothes), but we were always clean. Many mornings she would hunt rabbits or squirrels for our lunch. One morning, Mother found a small house to rent near the railroad tracks. She put Hank, me, and our few belongings on a wagon and started toward that little house. On the way, she stopped to mail a letter. A man walked up to her in the post office and said, 'I am Thaddeus B. Rose. I have a house you are welcome to rent free until you get on your feet.'" (*Irene Williams Smith in the* Washington Post, *January 1, 1993)*

"They came in an old flatbed truck with a bunch of beat-up furniture. It was called Rose Street for Thaddeus B. Rose. He'd worked for the railroad and had a little money. He'd dug out the red dirt from under the house to fill in a corner lot he owned and that left the house sitting up about four-and-a-half or five feet off the ground. Hank would get under there and yodel and play his guitar. Hank's mother was a practical nurse and she'd sometimes work nights, and she'd come to the edge of the porch and say 'Hiram, hush that noise.' He was called 'Hiram' or 'Harm' back then. He shined shoes and sold peanuts on the railroad platform in Georgiana, but they run him off 'cause it was dangerous. The Williamses had no money. Most Sundays after church, my mother would ask me to take a platter of roast chicken, pork chops, rice and gravy, and pie to them. ☞

Hank and Irene, left (circa 1926) and above

(continued from page 23)

Wednesday evenings, me and Hiram would sit on a board fence around their house and listen to the negro church, which was about a mile away. It was prayer meetin' night. The most beautiful music in the world. The breeze came from the south and it would undulate the sound. One minute soft, next minute loud, like it was orchestrated. One night, Hiram looked up at me and said, 'One day, I'm gonna write songs like that.'" *(Howard Sims, October 1998)*

"I been singing ever since I can remember. My mother was an organist in Mount Olive, Alabama, and my earliest memory is sittin' on that organ stool by her and hollerin'. I must have been five, six years old and louder'n anybody. I learned to play guitar from an old colored man. He was named Tee-Tot, and he played in a colored street band. I was shinin' shoes, sellin' newspapers, and followin' this ol' nigrah around to get him to teach me to play the guitar. I'd give him fifteen cents or whatever I could get hold of for a lesson. When I was about eight years old, I got my first guitar. A second-hand $3.50 guitar my mother bought me." *(Hank Williams interviewed by Ralph J. Gleason in the* San Francisco Chronicle*)*

"I'll never forget the day I brought Hank home his first guitar, a second-hand instrument that cost $3.50. That was a lot of money then. I was making only a quarter a day nursing or sewing. Hank was so overjoyed at the sight of the guitar, he rushed out in the yard and grabbed a calf by the tail. The little animal threw him and broke his arm, and he couldn't play his new guitar for weeks." *(Lillie Williams in* Life Story of Our Hank Williams—the Drifting Cowboy, *Philbert Publications, Montgomery, Alabama, 1953)*

"We moved to Greenville, Alabama, when Hank was about eight. He often heard a roving band, three black men who used to go from house to house playing guitar, fiddle, and a bass made with a tub and broomstick. The leader of the band, guitarist Rufus Payne, was nicknamed Tee-Tot. Hank would follow him every step of the way, begging him to teach him to play. Tee-Tot called Hank 'Little White Boss,' and finally because Mother became afraid that Hank would get lost or hurt, she asked Tee-Tot to give Hank music lessons in exchange for food." *(Irene Williams Smith in the* Washington Post, *January 1, 1993)*

"Tee-Tot lived a little ways out of town. He taught Hank chords and taught me chords, but the first chords we ever learned my mother [Alice McNeil] showed us. My mother could play banjo, guitar and piano, and Lillie had a good voice. Real strong. She sent Hank to singing school out from Georgiana, a gospel, shaped-note singing school. He went to that, a little old country church. Hank had the talent, they didn't. Even then, he would get up and sing a song without any music at all." *(Hank's cousin J. C. McNeil, June 5, 1992)*

"Tee Tot had a street band. They made their living playing up and down the street, passing the hat for collection. Hank began to follow them everywhere, begging Tee-Tot to teach him just one more chord. I can still hear Tee-Tot say, 'Please, little white boss, run away. Dis ole man is tired. Can't teach you today.' But Hank was persistent. When Hank was [thirteen], we moved to Montgomery where there were more opportunities for mother to earn a living. She began to run a boarding house. Our mother was the most dynamic woman I have ever known. If you made her angry, you had a wildcat on your hands, yet she could be as gentle as a lamb. For one of her children or for a friend, she would turn the world upside down." *(Irene Williams in manuscript of* My Life with a Treasured Brother, *circa 1971)*

Tee-Tot's death certificate

I wish I had a dad

I guess I'm aful lucky, my mother says I
am   she say's why son you have a lot
and I reply yes mam, I've got a knife
I've got a bike I got a dog named Tad
I've got a lot of comic books I've got a drawing pad
I've a ray roger _____ I aint doing bad
But if I really _____ ish I'd rather have
a dad.
The dad I've go _____ ___mes but once a
year I ask h _____ stayed away and he
said looked a _____ to take my
mind away by pulling at my ear
mom wasn't there she never is when papa
pays a call   when she came back I tried
to talk But mom said thats all
But theirs my dog an every soon I tell it
all to Tad he ask me what its like to hav

I wish I had a dad

I guess I'm aful lucky, my mother says I
am she says why son you have a lot
and I reply yes mama, I've got a knife
I've got a bike I got a dog named Tad
I've got a lot of comic books I've got a drawing pad
I've a roy rogers gun oh I aint doing bad
But if I really had my wish I'd rather have
a dad.
The dad I've got you see he comes but once a
year I ask him why he stayed away and he
said look a here and tried to take my
mind away by pulling at my ear
mom wasn't there she never is when papa
pays a call when she come back I tried
to talk But mom said thats all
But there's my dog an every sore I tell it
all to tad he ask me what its like to have
a real live dad for one whole day
and I reply its lots of fun and then he
wags his tail like he wish he had one
you report card must be signed by you parents
The teacher said one day

and so I threw the card away
cause other kids have parents all I have is
mom and she all rite I love her heap
But a mom is just a mom
the boys I got to school with get lickings when...
from their dad's I havent had such lickens
but ye I wish I had
nex year when he comes to see me I'll say papa
whale me please But I bet I never get him
to not even if I tease, last time we played
and romped a lot you never saw such fun
that day he took me hunting and let me
shoot the gun, But when he said what do
you wont that till now you havent had
I said you was it and could you be again
I wont a full time dad
I guess I'm realy luck my mother says I
am she says why son you have a lot and
I reply yes mom, I've got a horse I've got a
kite I've got a stream line schatter
I've got a bow and arrow set I've got a sling shot
shatter I've got a roy rogers gun oh I aint doing bad
but if I really had my wish I'd rather have a dad

From Hank's notebook:
His handwritten lyrics to "I Wish I Had a Dad"

"I went to the Naval Hospital in Pensacola for a short time, then to the Veterans Hospital in Alexandria, Louisiana, where I stayed seven years until January 1937. I was at Gulfport, Mississippi, until August 1938, out until October, when I went back. I spent Christmas with the children then went back and stayed 'til April 1939, when I was discharged. During my long hospital period, it was reported in some parts that I was dead. On seeing some of my old acquaintances afterward, they looked at me as if seeing a ghost." *(Lon Williams, undated letter to* The Progressive Era, *Camden, Alabama)*

Lillie was preoccupied with making a living, and Hank grew up a solitary child, frequently sick. The proximity of his extended family couldn't quite compensate for Lon's disappearance or for a physical disability that, according to Lon, manifested itself as a raised spot on Hank's spine. He found solace in music, probably recognizing that he didn't have the physical strength to work in the lumber mills or on the farm. Hank was fifteen by the time Lon finally left the V.A. hospital system. Lon moved to McWilliams, Alabama, where Hank would go see him when he played in the area.

Hank and Irene

Irene (top left) and Hank (second from right) with their cousin Bernice McNeil (bottom right). Remainder unknown.

Lillie (second from left, top row) with Hank (middle, bottom row) and his cousin Bernice McNeil (lower right)

"THE WPA BLUES"

Hank was thirteen when the family moved to Montgomery in July 1937. By then, Lillie had found that she liked the rooming house business, and Hank had already made it clear that he wanted to be a musician. There were better opportunities for both of them in Alabama's state capital, then a city of 72,000 people. Lillie had Hank and Irene on the streets hawking peanuts and packed lunches. Hank would often set up in front of what was then the only local radio station, WSFA, selling whatever Lillie had prepared, shining shoes, and playing his guitar. On more than one occasion he was brought up to the studio to perform, and the program director, Caldwell Stewart, once claimed to have run a remote microphone to the street to capture "The Singing Kid."

Hank began performing on WSFA as early as 1937 or 1938 and got his own show in 1941. This photo was probably taken around that time.

Hank, Hezzy Adair, and Braxton Schuffert formed the original
Drifting Cowboys around 1938. L-R: Hezzy, Hank, fiddle player
Freddie Beach, and Braxton

"When Hank was [thirteen], we moved to Montgomery where he sang his first original song in public. It was called 'The WPA Blues.' Since most of the audience worked for the WPA [President Franklin D. Roosevelt's Works Progress Administration] at the time, they laughed and stormed. Hank got the $15 prize. He took the money and set up all his school friends. He never stopped doing that. When Hank was in the chips, so were his friends, as long as the money held out. Always." (*Lillie Williams,* Life Story of Our Hank Williams—the Drifting Cowboy, *Philbert Publications, Montgomery, Alabama, 1953)*

"Hank was fifteen when I met him. He looked older 'n that. He was tall and had a voice on him like a grown man—strong, clear. He just sang straight notes, no breaking notes. His mother told me that she couldn't get him away from the radio when I was on every morning 6:00 to 6:30. I met Hezzy Adair coming back from doing a radio show one morning. He come down Bell Street chokin' a harp. He could play 'Fox Chase,' 'Lost John,' all those. I was playing a guitar and I said, 'Boy, can you play with a guitar?' He said, 'Hell yes,' so I said he should come up the house and we'd play some. His mother was dead and his dad was a roving sign painter, rode a bicycle. Hezzy was on his own. When he started playing with Hank some, he stayed with Mizz Williams. Hank was still in school then, but he skipped school a lot. A boy who went to school with him said that Hank was asleep on his arm. He asked the teacher if he should wake him up, and the teacher said, 'Naw, don't wake him up, he ain't gonna learn anything anyway.' All he studied was music. He was trying to write songs even then." (*Braxton Schuffert, one of the original Drifting Cowboys, December 16, 1992)*

L-R: Pee Wee Moultrie, Charlie Mays,
Sue Taylor, Hezzy Adair, Hank

"Our first fiddle player was Freddie Beach, then we had Mexican Charlie Mays, 'cept he didn't look like no Mexican to me, but he was a good fiddle player. Charlie, Hank, Irene, Hezzy Adair, and me played for a theater chain. We played a while in Roanoke, Alabama. Hank's mother had a '38 or '39 Ford station wagon that we went up there in. We played at three, six, and nine o'clock, then drove the hundred miles back to Montgomery for seventy-five dollars. We was rich—fifteen bucks apiece less gas.

"There used to be an old big garage down near the Civic Center. We played for a dance marathon. People would dance 'til they fell out. They could go to the restroom, get them a coffee or a hot dog, but they couldn't lay down or sit down. We played every night that whole time. No microphones. We'd sing loud enough you could hear us clear 'cross the auditorium. That's the way we played dances then. We put the piano in the middle of the floor, we'd gather round the piano and play. When we started playing together Mizz Williams ordered black hats for all the guys and white hats for the girls. I had a '35 V-8 Ford. That thing would burn as much oil as gas. I'd carry a five-gallon oil can in the trunk. I'd step on the gas and people behind me couldn't see nothing. My brother was a mechanic for Hormel and I'd get him to save me the oil from the oil changes. We'd book schoolhouses. The school would run people in the buses. The school would get thirty percent and we'd get seventy percent. Admission was fifty cents. Most times, we'd be lucky to come out with enough to buy guitar strings and gas." (*Braxton Schuffert, December 16, 1992*)

The line-up of the Drifting Cowboys was rarely stable. For a year or two the band included accordionist Pee Wee Moultrie. Both Pee Wee and Braxton Schuffert confirm that Lillie played a very active role in Hank's career, arranging and advertising show dates, collecting money at the door, and paying the band members. Hank had started drinking at age eleven and by his late teens was already prone to binges. The Drifting Cowboys remember Lillie "riding herd" on him, trying to prevent him from drinking before show dates, often to no avail.

"While playing a radio program, I noticed two individuals watching us. They identified themselves as 'Hank and Hezzy.' They said they had a band called 'Hank and Hezzy and the Drifting Cowboys.' For some reason, Hezzy's name was dropped, but he continued playing bass. We moved into Mrs. Williams' boarding house on Perry Street. We started a radio show on WCOV and a Saturday night barn dance at Fort Dixie Graves Armory. A man who owned a string of theaters in Georgia, Alabama, and Florida wanted us to perform but wanted a girl singer, so we went out and found one [Sue Taylor]. Hank was on his best behavior the first two weeks. The third week, we pulled into a town in south Alabama and went to the theater. The owner pulled out a bottle of peach brandy. We offloaded the car and Hank and Hezzy went off in search of some more booze. They both got loaded. Hank started the show and told the people that he wished he'd been born in their town and if it happened again, he'd make sure it happened there. He lost his pick and was strumming his guitar with his knuckles. Hezzy walked off to the west wing and vomited. People sitting on the left side could see him and started walking out. I figured they would run us out of town, but the manager was laughing his head off. He said it was the funniest thing he'd ever seen." (Former Drifting Cowboy Pee Wee Moultrie, 1995)

(top) Hank and his vocal partner, Sue Taylor
(bottom) Hank and Pee Wee Moultrie

(top) Hank and Juanealya, Pappy Neil McCormick's daughter, Panama City, Florida, April 24, 1941

(bottom) photo booth shot

"In 1940, a small group of people stayed at the boarding house on the way to a rodeo or carnival [in Texas and Mexico]. Hank took off with them and left his band sitting there cooling their heels, so we started working with another local band led by Dad Crysel. Hank came back a short time later, claiming he had back trouble. He wanted his band back. Mr. J. L. Frank [country star Pee Wee King's father-in-law/manager] would frequently come to town representing the Opry Artist Service Bureau. He'd rent the city auditorium for a Sunday show and use us to do his legwork. Then he'd bring in Opry stars, like Roy Acuff, and let us do the show with them. We usually got a better response than his Opry folks. Drunk or sober, Hank had the uncanny ability to hold an audience's attention. By 1940, Hank's drinking problem was getting worse. All we were getting was three meals a day, and most of the money was going to Hank's mother." (*Pee Wee Moultrie, 1995*)

The trip to Texas and Mexico was the first of many times that Hank would try to escape Montgomery, leaving his band members stranded there. After arguing with Lillie, Hank would often go to Pensacola, Florida. Holed up in the San Carlos Hotel, he would perform with Pappy Neil Cormick's Hawaiian Troubadours, who broadcast over WCOA, located in the hotel.

Hank was unable to keep a band together after the United States entered World War II in December 1941. Gas rationing made travel difficult, and the draft depleted the pool of musicians. Classified 4-F, unfit for active service, Hank went to the Kaiser Shipyard in Portland, Oregon, to work as a welder in the Liberty shipbuilding program. He stayed just two months, returning to Montgomery in August or September 1942. Still unable to reassemble the Drifting Cowboys, he moved to Mobile, Alabama, in November to work for the Alabama Dry Dock and Shipbuilding Company.

"Hank was down in Mobile by hisself. He was staying with Uncle Bob Skipper on Monroe Street. Uncle Bob was renting from a lady that owned the house. Hank would hit the joints at night. Tried to get a band together when he was in the shipyards. It was in his blood. I would venture to say that he didn't work more than two or three months all told. He probably slept on the job more than anything else. It was encouraged by the foreman so that he could stretch the hours he could bill." (*Hank's cousin J. C. McNeil, June 4, 1992*)

Handley Texas
nov, 18th 1940
P.O. Box 478

Dear Mother,
I just got your letter
was glad to hear from you.
Mother the reason that jack
has not sent you any money ds
because he just bought 60 o wort
of cowboy suits + bootts for all
of us. he also has bought a ranch
where we are now. so he is short
one money, mother if there is any
way you can keep the card keep it if
you want to. I just singed a contract
with the Fort worth Rodeio officals
to advertise the Rodeio ove the air
for them this starts in the middle of
Oct. that will mean 50 a week for
me, and I will send you some money
I wrote you a letter 2 days bfore I wrote
the card. I all so sent you a letter
wich a $5 bill in it did you get this
ore not. Tell drene I wrote her
a letter.

didn't she get it. Tell Euylen
I said to behave her self.
Tell dren to go all pic. men
and gine him my addres
I tell him to write to
me also ask him if he
got a letter from me I wrote
him one. Tell drene to forget that
band ddia for the present time & I will
be back in about 7 months with a
Real band & pleantly of money to.
Run one on. Tell Euylen to gine
the bids at the Strond my new
addres + Tell them to write to
me. this is the plates country I world
Texas. Tell Jim + Pauline the Reason
I have not wrote them is because
I lost the address. Tell Britt I said
hello. also Tell Pll will. + jimiey wickerson
I said to be Ready to come at any time
I call them. Tell drene not to worry
that those I hit out fits around there are
not making any money. so tell Euey
body hello + to break dow I will
to me. Love Hank x x
x x x x x x x x x x x x x x x

In 1940, Hank left Montgomery with a rodeo headlined
by Juan Lobo (aka Jack Wolf). Here, he writes home
with detailed instructions for everyone, and apologies
for not sending any money.

Dear Mother.

How are you this morning. I am pretty tired. we had lots of excitement yesterday at the yard. I told Irene about it. she will tell you about it. I got your letter. sure was glad to hear from you. did you see Jimmie tell him those shoes he gave me sure are comeing in handy. I am sending the rest of the money on my watch in this letter, please send it to me at once for I need it. tell me when you are comeing down I sure would like to see you. you can send those gloves to

if you will and mother send me a picture of my old band and ask Irene can I borrow that big picture of my self and song book. I need them. I am on the radio at WALA every wensday morning at 6 45 see if you can get wensday. I am going to do a song for you and Irene. I have a friend down here who has a Recording machine I have made some records and I have wrote some new songs. will send you a record of them.
        Write soon
            Love
            Hank

Although Hank writes in this letter to Lillie of working on the radio station WALA, he was probably dismissed. When he returned to Mobile later in his career, he was invited by WALA to sing live on-air. In front of the station staff, he told the program director, "When I was in Mobile before, I tried to get on this station. I wasn't good enough then, and I reckon I still ain't good enough."

Teenage Hank

The Ga-Ana Theater in Georgiana, Alabama, where
Hank often performed early in his career

(above, right) Hank, possibly with his
first cousin, Dorothy Dobbins

(right) Circa 1938

"Hank was nineteen [in 1942] when he gave up all hopes
of ever making the big-time as singer. He just left for Mobile and
got a job in the shipyards. But I believed in Hank, so I rented a car
and went to every schoolhouse and nightclub in the Montgomery
area. I booked Hank solid for sixty days. Then I went to Mobile
and got him and put him back in it. When Hank saw the datebook
for those shows, he gave me the sweetest smile I've ever seen and
said, 'Thank God, mother, you have made me the happiest boy in
the world.'" (*Lillie Williams in* Life Story of Our Hank Williams—the
Drifting Cowboy, *Philbert Publications, Montgomery, Alabama, 1953)*

(top, left) With an unidentified friend, late 1930s

(top, middle) With his cousin Dorothy Dobbins

(top right and immediate left) Hank on a family vacation to South Carolina, 1938

(far left) Hank and the Drifting Cowboys, circa 1940. L-R: unknown announcer, "Indian" Joe Hatcher, "Mexican" Charlie Mays, Lillie, Hank, Boots Harris, unknown, Shorty Seals

3 "THIS AIN'T NO PLACE FOR ME"

In early 1943 Hank returned to Montgomery to work as a musician. Unable to reassemble the Drifting Cowboys, Hank joined a medicine show touring south Alabama. It was there that he met his first wife, Audrey Sheppard Guy. She was married to a serviceman and had a two-year-old daughter, Lycrecia Ann. Audrey, like Lillie, provided much of the ambition that Hank lacked.

Audrey, Hank, and Lycrecia

Never happier—Hank and Audrey, Alabama, 1944

"I met Hank in Banks, Alabama. He was working a medicine show. My dad's only sister was with me, and it was her idea to stop and see what was going on. I said, 'I never heard of Hank Williams before,' but I learned later that a lot of people in the area *had* heard of him. I said, 'This guy will be number one on the Grand Ole Opry one of these days.' I had that feeling very strongly. Anyway, after the show was over, Hank and these other people were going around selling herbs. Little vials. He came up to the car. I'll never forget how country he talked. He said, 'Ma'am, don't you think you need some of these herbs?' then he quickly looked back and he said, 'No, I don't believe you do.' My aunt asked him what he was gonna do after the show, and he said, 'Well, I have no plans.' She said, 'Well, would you like to go with us?' So he went with us after the show that night, and we went to a little club. I just seemed to be with him from then on. I just wanted to help him. Though I had no experience in the business, I felt this guy had a tremendous talent. I'll tell you something: If some woman, equally as strong as I am, had not come along, there would never have been a Hank Williams. He did not want to live when I met him. He was an alcoholic.

"I'm kinda psychic. I had a brother who was ten years old and I was twelve. He was disgustingly healthy, but I knew for months he was gonna die. Then he went hunting with my dad one afternoon and came in and took double pneumonia. They were bringing in doctors and nurses, and I was thinking to myself, 'You can bring Jesus Christ himself, and he will not live.' That's how strong I believed it. That's how strong I believed in Hank. He was lucky with a God-given talent, and I was lucky with a few brains, so I used to go out and book shows....I took up money [at] the door, then I'd go up onstage with him. He used to do a blackface act that was just outasight. He'd sing a little bit, then do a few funnies.

"When I first met Hank he kept saying, 'I want to tell you. There's something I want to tell you.' Each time, he'd back out. Finally, one day we were at my dad's and we were sitting on the grass, and I said, 'Hank, you've got to tell me what it is on your mind.' He said, 'It's my mother.' I was so innocent then, I didn't know if she was dead. He said, 'I want to take you home and introduce you to her,' then he said, 'You know what she's gonna say when she meets you? She's gonna say, "Where did you meet this whore?"' I said, 'Hank, your mother couldn't possibly say that. I know she couldn't.' You know, we walked in, and that's the first thing she said. I ran back to the car. Hank and [his] mother fought like men would fight. I tell you, *she* was his trouble. Like I said, when I met him, he didn't want to live, and he was like eighteen or nineteen." (*Audrey Williams, interviewed by Dorothy Horstman, 1973*)

(opposite, above) L-R: Lum York, Sammy Pruett, Hank, unknown, Audrey, Jimmy Webster. Many of these musicians would work with Hank on and off in the years ahead, with the exception of Jimmy Webster, who was killed in a car wreck while in Hank's employment, around 1945.

(opposite, below) On July 10, 1942, Lillie finally divorced Lon, and, one week later, took out a license to marry a man named Homer Haatchett, although it's unclear if they actually married. Three months later, on September 10, 1942, Lillie married a Cajun serviceman, J. C. Bozard. They are seen here with Hank and Audrey.

In November 1943, Hank and Audrey returned to Mobile to work as welders, staying two-and-a-half months before returning to Montgomery to assemble a band. Steel guitarist Don Helms and electric guitarist Sammy Pruett, both of whom would later work with Hank in Nashville, first joined the Drifting Cowboys in 1944.

"We were supposed to meet Hank at Art Freehling's music store, but he wasn't there. We went outside and I saw this real long-legged guy coming. He walked up, and he said, 'Y'all the group?' We said, 'Yeah.' He said, 'Well, I'm Hank Williams, follow me.' We walked round the corner and down the block to a hock shop. He said, 'Jake, you got any more of them blackjacks in there?' and there was a tray of 'em. He passed 'em out, he said, 'Boys, if y'all gonna play with me, by God you're gonna need these.' He wasn't kiddin' either." (*Don Helms, 1992*)

"One night we was playing a dance at a juke joint, and there was a poppin' sound and someone come up and said there was a fella out there shootin' with a gun. Directly, he come in. He was wearin' overalls—no shirt—and he had a big ol' loaded pistol and one of them bullets hit a heater and richocheted 'round the room. Man, you talk about huntin' a table. Another place down near Fort Deposit they had chicken wire out front of the bandstand so if they started throwing bottles they wouldn't hit the band." (*Drifting Cowboy R. D. "Sonny" Norred, June 1992*)

Hank and the Drifting Cowboys found a steady gig at the Riverside Club in Andalusia, Alabama, and moved there, as did Audrey. She also filed for divorce from her husband, Erskine Guy, promising to marry Hank if he straightened up.

"I knew Hank about a year before I married him. All that time, he was trying to get me to marry him. I was hesitant because he had a drinking problem, and I'd never been around anyone with a drinking problem. He was living in a trailer in Andalusia and playing a club, a rather large club, in Andalusia. I was doing the cooking for the boys. All of a sudden one afternoon, he asked me, and I said 'Yes.' He'd been doing real good, not drinking. We went by the justice of the peace, who ran a filling station, with a couple of the boys in the band, and we got married. It was December 15, 1944." *(Audrey Williams on* Hank Williams…Reflections by Those Who Loved Him, *MGM Records, 1975)*

(above) Possibly the wedding photo, December 1944

(opposite) Hank and Audrey

Out there in the lonely church yard
she's waited so long for me
And soon I know I'll be with her
her dear face once more to see

Then god will welcome us together
to our new home so sweet and fair
he will straighten my old bent body
and wipe the grey from my hair

up there well be young and happy
With jesus in the skie
Where all is love and happness
and well never again have to say good

so don't grieve and mourn for me
When I go don't cry my friends when
I've waited so long for this day
to meet her once again.

(The old man's Last good by))
The day was slowly dying
With it a man bent and old
he called his friends to him
and to them this story he told

The years have been long an lonely,
little happness I have known
for many year ago
God called the one that I loved home

all I had left was memories
of a love so true and divined
but sone it will all be over
I'm leaving it all behind.

(above, left) Hank and the Drifting Cowboys, 1945.
L-R: Lum York, Audrey, Louis Brown, Hank, Red Todd,
Jimmy Webster

(above, right) Welcomed back to WSFA by program
director Caldwell Stewart

"The weekend that the gig ended in Andalusia, Hank got drunk and Audrey pitched a fit. Hank threw her clothes in the mud in front of the trailer. She called the police and had him put in jail. I had to go get him out. I was embarrassed, but I went back in there. He was sitting on a bench in his cell, watching me. I didn't know what to say, but he was starin' at me. He said, 'What do you want me to do? Stand on my darn head?' I paid the thirty dollars and got him out. One of the policemen said, 'Come back 'n' see us, Hank.' He said, 'All of you can go to Hell.'" *(Don Helms, 1992)*

After the war, Hank reestablished himself on WSFA, Montgomery, quickly becoming one of the most popular singers in the city. The station frequently tried to dismiss him for unreliability, but the public always demanded his return.

Look! Look! Look!

BOYS AND **GIRLS**

BIG! BIG!

CHRISTMAS CANNED FOOD PICTURE SHOW PARTY

THIS COMING SATURDAY MORNING, 10 A.M.

PARAMOUNT THEATRE

ON THE STAGE **Hank Williams** and his WSFA Radio Gang

ON THE SCREEN Johnny Weissmuller & Brenda Joyce in **TARZAN** AND THE AMAZONS

—ADMISSION—

JUST A CAN OF FOOD

Help the needy on Christmas! Come to this picture show party and bring a can of food. All food will be distributed to the needy of Montgomery by the Salvation Army. Bring a real good can of something good to eat and help make this a Merry Christmas for everyone.

Remember the Date! This Coming Saturday Morning 10 A.M. (Doors open at 9:30 at the Paramount Theater). Come Early. Bring A Friend.

Sponsored By The Advertiser-Journal, The Paramount Theater, and Radio Station WSFA.

"Fans? I got a mob of 'em up here every morning and every afternoon. Some come from fifty miles! A lady from Opelika wrote me just this mornin'. She says, 'Say Hank, how much do it cost to come up and hear you sing? If it don't cost too much, we may come up there.' If anybody in my business knew as much about their business as the public did, they'd be alright. Just lately, somebody got the idea nobody didn't listen to my kinda music. I told ever'body on the radio this was my last program. 'If anybody's enjoyed it, I'd like to hear from 'em.' I got 400 cards and letters that afternoon and the next mornin'. They decided they wanted to keep my kinda music." *(Hank Williams in the* Montgomery Advertiser, *April 4, 1948)*

At the war's end, Chicago was considered the hub of the country record business. There were no recording studios in Nashville, no session men, and just one music publisher, Acuff-Rose Publications (a partnership between Hank's idol, Roy Acuff, and Tin Pan Alley songsmith Fred Rose). In the years immediately after the war, though, the country music business quickly centered upon Nashville. Hundreds of Saturday-night barndances were broadcast on local radio, but thirty minutes of Nashville's Grand Ole Opry were aired coast-to-coast on NBC radio, making the Opry a magnet for the biggest names in the business. At Audrey's insistence, Hank began looking toward Nashville and Acuff Rose.

"I knew about Fred Rose, and I knew that he had started a publishing company with Roy Acuff. I knew that Fred had written some pretty good songs, and I felt that he could maybe help Hank. So we called and set up an appointment. It was at WSM radio station, studio B. It was for one o'clock, but I don't remember the day. The nearer the time came, the more Hank backed out. He said, 'I ain't going. I ain't gonna let him hear my songs.' I said, 'You're going if I have to push you every inch of the way.' I just literally made him go. That day, Fred took four of Hank's songs, and we were just so happy and delighted, but Fred said, 'Boy, I don't know if you wrote these songs, whether you bought them off somebody. I don't know how you might have got 'em. I tell you what I want you to do. I'm gonna give you a title and I want you to go back home and write a song to it.' This song was 'Mansion on the Hill.' Hank worked and worked at that song, but he couldn't really get it together. The pressure was on him, and it wasn't really his idea. One night, we'd gotten through with dinner and washed up the dishes. I just sat down in the little kitchen there and I started humming 'Down in the Valley,' so I sat there and wrote that thing out and went into the living room, and Hank liked it, so we took it to Fred Rose. I never wanted Fred to know that Hank didn't write that song 'cause I was trying desperately to get him started." *(Audrey Williams interviewed by Dorothy Horstman, 1973)*

Fred Rose with Hank's guitarist, Sammy Pruett, to the left

Hank Williams Rides On Down Trail Of National Popularity On Air Records

By William E. Cleghorn

Local scenes and local people are featured in many songs written by Hank Williams, Montgomery's happy, roving cowboy.

"Move It Over," latest hit by Hank and his Drifting Cowboys is now running fourth among the nations most played juke box folk records, according to The Billboard.

Hank, popular musical artist and long time favorite in his home town, has been airing cowboy ballads, love songs, plaintive hill ditties and sacred hymns over Montgomery radio stations since 1936.

The spur-jangling Sinatra of the Western Ballad has written 23 songs published by Acuff and Rose, Nashville, but he never hit the jack pot until "Move It Over" moved him up.

That M-G.M. platter broke the

Hank Williams

100,000 mark in less than two months.

Based on a couple's disagreement, the song winds its way through fusses and fights with the old man ending up in the doghouse.

Waits for Inspiration

"Where the inspiration for that song came from, I couldn't say," Hank admitted. It wasn't his own married life. Mr. and Mrs. Hank Williams lead a model domestic life.

'Miss Audrey,' his wife, is the featured vocalist with the band." Hank taught her how to sing after their marriage. 'Miss Au-

drey' is a native of Pike County.

"I have been living in Montgomery so long that I call it home. We are building our home here,' he said.

Large radio stations in other sections of the country have gone after Hank now that his popularity has become nation wide, but he likes it here at WSFA and expects to stay.

Good Manager

Hank mentioned Bill Hamm, WSFA commercial manager, as one of his closest friends and one man who has helped him a great deal.

The Decca Company made Hank an offer recently, but he is loyal to M-G-M and the Acuff-Rose publishing house.

Hank says that Roy Acuff, the Tennessee Troubadour, and Fred Rose, song writer, have done much for him. Rose is Hank's personal recording manager.

Home town folk are plugging Hank for the movies. They claim he would be a natural for Western shows. Slim, quiet and nice looking, he has a large following among the younger set in these parts.

White Sombrero

Always seen with a white sombrero and with a white scarf knotted at the throat, Hank speaks and looks the part of a happy, roving cowboy.

Another big hit by Hank is "Pan American" written about the L&N train that leaves Montgomery each day headed for New Orleans.

He hopes to see "Move It Over" right at the top. Number one now is "Smoke Smoke Smoke", the famed weed song, by Tex

Williams. Number two is "Timtayshun," which Red Ingle and Jo Stafford shoved up the line. In third spot is "It's a Sin" by Eddy Arnold and His Tennessee Plowboys.

Religious Songs

Two of Hank's religious songs on records are "When Wealth Won't Save Your Soul" and "When God Comes and Gathers His Jewels."

Singing in a lusty backwoods style, with the fiddlers and guitars of his drifting cowboys, Hank sings his songs in spirited tempo. Hank's next record release will be "Fly Trouble".

Hank writes all kinds of songs, but he says the juke songs go best. A juke song is—well, "Move It Over" is a juke song.

Hank, deeply religious himself, likes hymns and sings at least one on his daily 4 p.m. program.

Takes 30 Minutes

When it comes to writing songs, Hank whips them out in about 30 minutes if the idea is good. And if the idea is not good, Hank soon knows and discards it.

As for a song, Hanks says you will never know how it will go until it has been released for about three months.

Hank and the Drifting Cowboys spend part of their week playing at school houses, dances, theaters, and shows.

The well-known theme song of the cowboys, "Happy Roving Cowboy," is an indication of their cheerful nature.

Fred Rose placed Hank with a small New York–based label, Sterling Records. The first of four Sterling records appeared in January 1947. In March, Rose negotiated a contract with the newly launched MGM Records. "Decca, Columbia, all the big ones. They heard about Hank and was trying to sign him up," remembered Audrey. "He almost went with Decca, but the way I felt about it, Decca had Ernest Tubb and Red Foley, and MGM was just starting. I said to Hank, 'Why don't we go with MGM and build with them?'" Hank's first hit, "Move It on Over," came with his first MGM record in the spring of 1947.

"We built the Journey's Inn and opened May 6, 1946. Soon after that, Hank came by. He and his boys played one night a week for dances. He told me one time, 'You and I are both poor boys trying to get a start, but some day I expect to have some real money rolling in.' I asked what he meant, and he said, 'I've just signed a contract to make records in Nashville. It won't amount to much at first, but after a year or so I will really be in the money.' We worked on an 80:20 basis. Many times the receipts were only about fifty dollars, and I wouldn't take my cut as I knew it cost them at least that much to come from Montgomery. He composed a piece called 'The Journey's Inn Blues' and sang it over the radio in Montgomery. He'd say the Journey's Inn was in Camden, Alabama, and he'd be there on a certain night. People for miles around would come to hear him, and he could hardly leave when his time was up. The young folks would always beg him to play one more. His father from McWilliams would always be there to boost him on. He played here about two years." (*Henry B. Hawthorne, Camden, Alabama, letter to* The Progressive Era, *undated*)

"'Move It on Over' is a No. 1 hillbilly hit and has already sold more than 108,000 records, which is also to say that Hillbilly Hank, who three times a day sings, chirps, brays or moans bouncy ditties over WSFA to the whangings of his guitar, is not getting any poorer. With three cents a copy pouring in from his sheet music, plus two cents a record for every recording, plus another half-cent a side for writing the things, he bids fair to become Montgomery's most successful composer. If things go right, he may pick up $15,000 or $20,000 in addition to the golden chicken feed he scratches for his three daily commercial programs on WSFA. This is why the boys around the studio, even the avowed haters of hillbilly music, get quiet and reverent when Hank looks like he might be even beginning to think of having another song idea. 'Shhh,' they say. 'That's Shakespeare. It used to be hillbilly, now it's Shakespeare.'" (*Allen Rankin in the* Montgomery Advertiser, *April 4, 1948*)

HILLBILLY HIT PARADE

(From a regional spot survey of record retailers and disc jockeys)

1.	SMOKE, SMOKE, SMOKE	Tex Williams
2.	MOVE IT ON OVER	Cowboy Copas, Grandpa Jones, Fairley Holden
3.	I'LL HOLD YOU IN MY HEART	Eddy Arnold
4.	DAUGHTER OF JOLE BLON	Johnny Bond
5.	ANSWER TO RAINBOW AT MIDNIGHT	Bill Carlisle
6.	TIMTAYSHUN	Red Ingle, Jo Stafford
7.	IT'S A SIN	Eddy Arnold
8.	THAT'S WHAT I LIKE ABOUT THE WEST	Tex Williams
9.	FEUDIN' AND FIGHTIN'	Dorothy Shay
10.	WHITE CHRISTMAS	Cowboy Copas

As was common at the time, several artists rushed to cover "Move It on Over." Three of the cover versions appear to have been more popular than Hank's, according to this chart, although Hank's record outranked the others on the industry standard *Billboard* chart.

MGM's New York–based engineers seemed less than impressed with what they clearly considered the bush-league recording quality of Hank's first MGM session—they labeled this master "spoiled." Fred Rose used the nucleus of Red Foley's band on this session in place of the Drifting Cowboys.

(R)

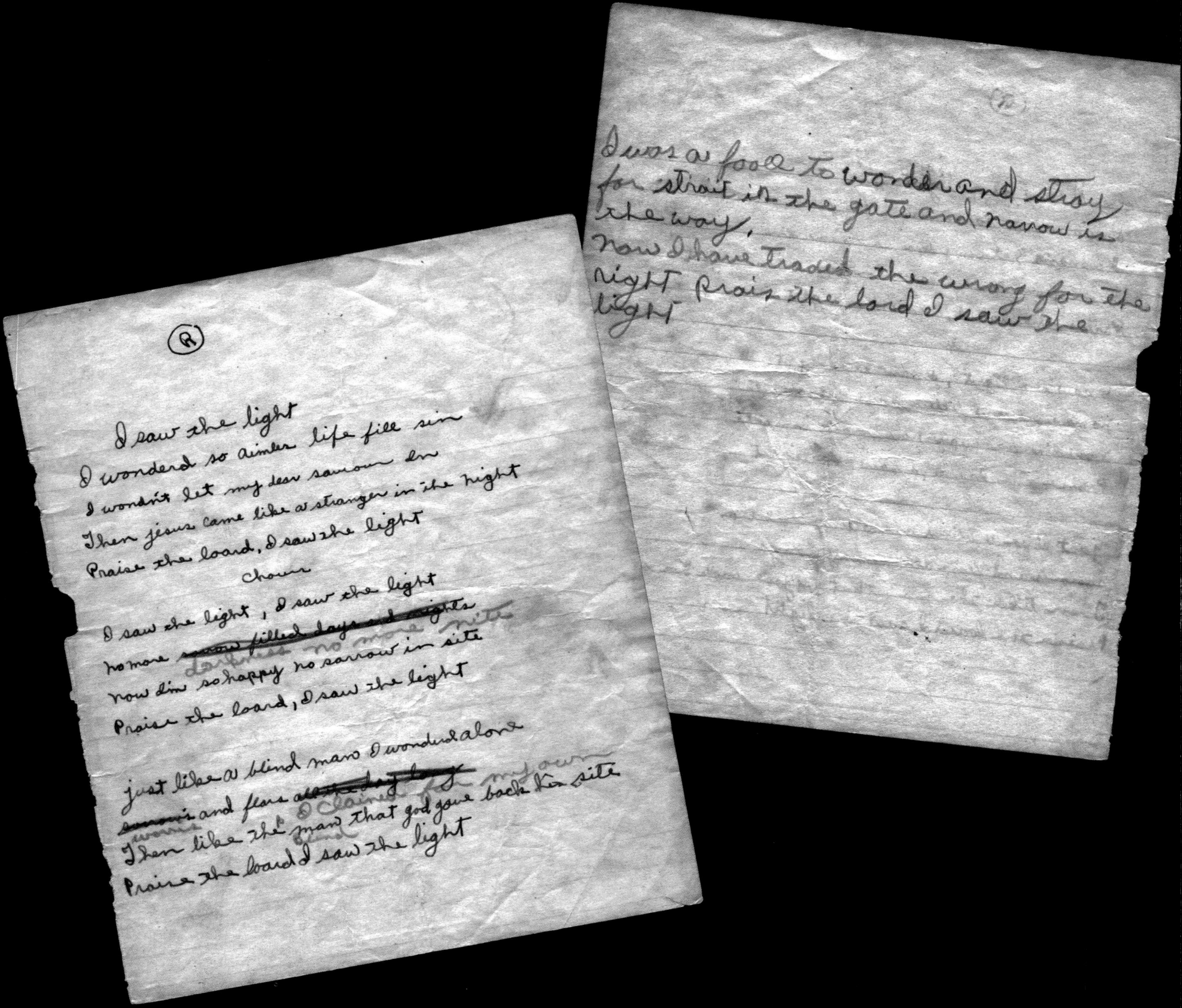

I saw the light

I wonderd so aimles life fille sin
I wouldn't let my dear saviour in
Then jesus came like a stranger in the night
Praise the loard, I saw the light

Chours

I saw the light, I saw the light
no more ~~sorrow filled days and nights~~ darkness no more nite
now I'm so happy no sarrow in site
Praise the loard, I saw the light

just like a blind man I wonderd alone
~~sorrows~~ worries and fears ~~all the day long~~ I claimed for my own
Then like the blind man that god gave back his site
Praise the loard I saw the light

(2)

I was a foole to wonder and stray
for strait is the gate and narrow is the way,
Now I have traded the wrong for the right Praise the lord I saw the light

(I saw the light)
Once I walked in darkness
didn't know wrong from right
Then I met my saviour
(Praise the loard) I saw the light,

Now my life is full of sunshine
my heart is free and light
Now I'm walking with jesus
(Praise the loard) I saw the light.

life is so free and happy
When you travel in the light
no more sorrow and fears
Praise the loard) I saw the light

just like a blind man
that has regained his site
now I know my saviour
(Praise the loard) I saw the light

Wondering so aimless in the darkness
day was just like nite
no hope for the hereafter (but
Praise the loard) I saw the light.

(Chor)
I saw the light, I saw the light
no more lonely days and nights
all met my saviour up in the skie
(Praise the lord) I saw the light

Jan 26, 1947

I SAW THE LIGHT
By Hank Williams

Two drafts of "I Saw the Light," one of them (this page) unpublished until now. "We played a show in Fort Deposit, Alabama, and Hank was higher than a kite by the time it was over. [Lillie Williams] drove home, and he was in the back seat sleepin' it off. There was a beacon light near Dannelly Field Airport, and Mizz Williams knew it always took time to get Hank awake when he was drunk like that, so she turned around and told him, 'Hank, wake up, we're nearly home. I just saw the light.' Between there and home he wrote the song." *(Montgomery musician Leabourne Eads, April 19, 1992)*

Hank and his cousin Marie Harvell
(right) and an unidentified friend,
Montgomery, circa 1944

Hank with Irene's son, John T. Smith Jr., April 17, 1944

I

I came to town the other day
Just to see what I coued see
and I here to tell you now
This aint no place for me

II

With all these light's & automobue's
folk's I just don't belong
I know a mule de stuborn
but me and him can get along

III

A girl stoped and picked me up
in big new shiney automobuel
The she looked at me and said
big boy you can Take the whell

IV

We started g down the road
and I toed that thing to go
and the next thing I knew
we had hit a big oak tree

V

I spraind my arm an bent my nose
and all most brake my neck
now folks If I had my mule
we woued'nt have had that wreck

VI

When I tell a mule to gee
I know hes going to turn right
but you can tell this cair to gee
an their so tell whire youve right

VII

Im going back to the country
and leave these poe crazy fooes
and frone now on when I ride
friend Ill be redeing on my mule.

oct 10. 1947

Hank at Taft Skipper's farm, Georgiana, Alabama, circa 1944

4 "THE 'LOVESICK BLUES' BOY": SPRING 1948—SPRING 1949

Hank was enjoying his fame in Montgomery but wanted to take the next step toward success in a larger market. At some point in 1947 or early 1948, he approached radio station WLAC in Nashville, hoping to join its on-air staff as a live performer, but word of his alcoholism had already reached Nashville, and he was rebuffed. He seemed moored in Montgomery despite healthy sales of his first MGM records and the climb of "Move It on Over."

```
FOLEY:    I'VE KNOWN SOME FISHERMEN IN MY LIFE, AND I'VE KNOWN SOME SINGERS,
          TOO..BUT I'VE NEVER KNOWN A MAN QUITE LIKE TONIGHT'S PRINCE
          ALBERT GUEST, WHO CAN'T MAKE UP HIS MIND WHETHER HE'D RATHER
          FISH THAN SING, OR SING THAN FISH.  BUT I CAN GUARANTEE YOU HE
          DOES BOTH ABOUT AS WELL AS THEY CAN BE DONE. I MEAN THAT GOOD OLE
          LOVE-SICK BLUES BOY, HANK WILLIAMS!  ...  (APPLAUSE) .. HANK,
          COME UP HERE AND TELL US ALL ABOUT YOURSELF. HEY, AIN'T THAT A
          NEW GUITAR YOU'VE GOT THERE?

HANK:     SURE IS RED..
```

I hope you shed a million tears

I

I gave my heart an soul to you
you done me rong so many years
yes I hope you suffer now
I hope you shed a million tears

II

I hope you dreams all fade an die
an you smiles all turn
all turn to fears
may you suffer same as me
I hope you shed a million tears

"Your friend, Fred Rose"

Hank and Audrey and several band members were living in Lillie's boarding house, but Audrey fought constantly with Lillie, and when the first royalty checks for "Move It on Over" arrived, Audrey insisted that Hank buy a small house. Better sensing Hank's potential than Hank himself, Audrey continually berated him for his drinking. In the spring of 1948, Hank's frustration and Audrey's impatience came to a head.

"Audrey run us off from their house. We was all practicing in there in the living room. It worried me dead 'cause Audrey had that little girl, and all she's buying was just two eggs and a little loaf of bread every morning. They were trying to put a song together, and Audrey was just whining and whining. Then Hank said, 'Fred, let's us try another song,' and Audrey went storming off into the bedroom and sent her little girl into the living room, and the little girl said, 'My momma says for you all to go home.' When we left, Hank was yellin' at her and screamin' at her like nothin' you ever heard. He hit her hard." *(Hank's band members Fred and Irella Beach, June 4, 1992)*

Hank's music publisher and producer, Fred Rose, took an avuncular interest in him. Rose had been a professional songwriter since the 1920s and had been an alcoholic before his conversion to Christian Science and subsequent move to Nashville. Clearly he saw something of himself in Hank Williams, and he tried to guide, sometimes goad, his young protégé. As Hank's life unraveled that spring, Rose tried to help, but he drew the line when he felt he was being exploited.

ACUFF-ROSE PUBLICATIONS

220 CAPITOL BLVD.
NASHVILLE 3, TENNESSEE
TELEPHONE 6-2851

WESLEY H. ROSE,
General Manager

February 18, 1948

Dear Hank:

Sometimes we humans act in a funny way when things are not going our way. We make plans and when anyone interferes with our plans we have nervous breakdowns because we think that drowning our sorrows will make us forget our troubles, but this has never worked and never will work because when we wake up next morning we still have our troubles plus a hangover that prevents us from thinking clear enough to think our way out of the problem that we thought our way into.

Hank, we live by rules and regulations (Principle) the same as your automobile. The Automobile Companies keeps your car running by, what they call,"factory specifications" and when your car gets away from these specifications it ceases to run and you take it to a mechanic who gets it back to "factory specifications" and "MAN" is the same way. You cannot hope to be successful while neglecting the Principle of health. The principle of success and all other secondary principles depend on the principle of LIFE because without life there is no such thing as success.

Don't let Audry pull the wool over your eyes by making you jealous. That is the first weapon a woman uses on a man she loves. Woman think they way to hold a man is to make the man think they are cheating and if the man is sucker enough to go for it, he is supposed to start drinking and become a tramp, these women want to be scalp collectors and see how many mens lives they can wreck, but they can always be crossed up by a man who uses common sense. All the man has to do, is know that, if his woman loves him, she will not be satisfied with any other man and , if she doesn't love him, he is a chump to want her. I think Audry loves you and that she is being very foolish try to hurt you but as the old saying goes "WE ALWAYS HURT THE ONE WE LOVE". The trouble with you kids is that, both of you want to be boss, Both of you have pride. Pride, is one of the most destructive lies on earth, it make people liars, it makes them pretend to be something they aren't, it ruins businesses, it breaks up homes, it is something we all should get rid of, as quick as possible, so we can enjoy the happiness of humility. The three hardest words in the English language to say are "I WAS WRONG" but when we do muster enough courage to say it, we feel a sense of victory, we find out we
(Cont.)

SONGS FOR HOME FOLKS
(SOLE SELLING AGENTS FOR MILENE MUSIC)

-2-

are big enough to admit our faults and give ourselves the opportunity to correct our mistakes, and at the same time reflect peace and happiness. We human beings are too busy seeking our own happiness at the expense of others and never find it, because happiness is something you give, not get. This is what Jesus tried to tell us when he said "IT IS BETTER TO GIVE, THAN TO RECEIVE". You watch out for Audry's happiness, and I know she will watch out for yours and you two kids will not be looking for happiness on the wrong road. Put your pride in your pocket, and love each other, that is what you promised to do, when you got married. A business that sells a customer one thing, and delivers another doesn't stay in business long. Try giving others happiness, strive to do it, and you will feel the great sense of victory, everyone of us was created to feel. "THE GREATEST VICTORY YOU WILL EVER GAIN, IS OVER YOURSELF"

If Audry wants you to wreck your life because of this misunderstanding, fool her, Show her you can be a success in spite of her and not because of her. Don't fall right into the trap she has set for you and use this misunderstanding for an excuse to wreck the opportunity you have before you, Just remember, "The man who has an excuse for his failure, is still a failure"

Live by the rules the Creator set down for you and you will be healthy, successful and happy. I know because I live as close to these rules as I know how and I am healthy, successfull and happy.

The Bible is not the kind of book we have been accustomed to think it is. It is a book of rules, Just like the arithmetic we used in school, it is the rules of addition and subtraction. When we learn these rules, the problems alway work out right and we get the right answer. Jesus raised the dead, overcame poverty, healed the sick, even raised Himself from the dead and told us we could do it too, if we trusted in His rules for doing it, He said "If you believe on me, the works that I do, you shall do, and even greater works than these shall ye do" but most of the people today are too lazy or too proud to look up these rules. I'm glad I looked up and found some of these rules because I know that everyone will have to do it sooner or later or live in worry, poverty, unhappiness, unhealthy and finally die and miss all the good things that were created for our pleasure.

Read this letter a few times and think it over.

I'm opening up my heart to you because I love you like my own son and you can call on me anytime when you are in a problem and I'll do anything within my power to help you help yourself.

I leave for Los Angeles today and will be away about three weeks but Wesley will know where I am at all times, if you need me.

"ONLY GAME FISH SWIM UPSTREAM"

I am enclosing a little "Peace Prayer" that I wish you would learn by heart. It has helped me lots when I felt disturbed.

Your friend,
Fred Rose
Fred Rose

March 18, 1948

Dear Hank,

I feel kinda let down today after receiving your call 'cause I knew you were drinking again and Hank that is something I refuse to go for because it only proves a man's weakness.

If you love Audry, why don't you try and straighten out and be man enough to tell her you love her and are willing to change. Both times I visited you folks, I noticed you bossing her around for my benefit, and I knew she would get filled up one of these days and get enough. If I talked to Lorene the way you talk to Audry, she would walk out in nothing flat and I wouldn't blame her one bit....

I'm writing you this way because I know YOU LOVE AUDRY more than you are willing to admit and you are taking the wrong way out, slopping up a lot of poison that makes you feel sorry for yourself and makes your friends disgusted with you. If you really want Audry back, get a haircut and buy a new suit, wash your face and throw that damn whiskey bottle out the window and become a man that she would be proud to have back.

I am trying to be your friend 'cause I know you need a friend. The guys that are drinking with you are not your friends, they just like the whiskey you buy, and when you run out of money they will leave you by yourself and tell everyone else you are a drunk. I know what I am talking about because I have gone through the same thing that you are going through now.

I know you can become a successful man if you will allow yourself to be one. If you think you want to straighten out and let me take care of your business as I have been doing, sign the enclosed contracts and have them notarized. If you feel sorry for yourself and keep drinking then just tear them up and forget the whole deal....

Please don't phone me when you are drinking as it only makes me feel I'm being let down by a guy I felt would never let me down. Think it over and read this letter when you are sober and you'll see that I'm trying to help you find yourself. I am...

Your friend,
Fred Rose

"(The Broken Marrige "

Only two short years have passed dear
since I heard the preacher say
I join you two in holy wed lock
you belong to each other now from this day

We swore then to love each other
and to never ever part
what has happend to the love we knew then
to day we are far apart

In the presents our saviour
we said that we'd be true
but we lied my darling
somethings happened to the love we knew

to day I saw you darling
with another by your side
It hurt me so my darling
that I went home and cried

When our lives here are over
an ore that judment day
if we are still apart dear
how big a debt will we have to pay.

Jan 19, 1947

Wonting to show how much I loved

Trying to fill your love wish

I ~~built your beautiful~~ ~~Dreemed and buit you~~ a fine home

For ~~This~~ you wonted above all

~~All this~~ to keep our love strong

A house of love to call our own

~~Each thing~~ ~~thing~~ you gave me was a lie

With ~~lies~~ you fooled my trusting heart

Frome the truth ~~you cant~~ escape

"I didn't build a house of love

But an evil mansion of hate   But a mansion filld with hate

~~Everybody meant but~~   I was just a fool in

I knowd you never did care   love

Not once was I in your heart   you deceived me at the start

You build ~~it~~ cruel and evil lie

~~for ~~again~~ and you at the start~~

you cant find joy in my grief

you will find this out all to late

love cant even live in a mansion

That was built with lies and hate

~~Others loved you little Home~~

Every one else neir bout gave

But to me you were sugar sweet   1950

~~and~~ yet hateing and hopeing night

your scheme would soon be complet

March 19, 1948

Dear Hank,

Wesley [Fred Rose's son and partner, Wesley Rose] tells me you called this morning for more money after me wiring you four hundred dollars just the day before yesterday…. We have gone as far as we can go at this time and cannot send you any more.

Hank I have tried to be a friend of yours but you refuse to let me be one. I feel that you are just using me for a good thing, and this is where I quit. You have been very unfair, calling the house in the middle of the night and I hope you will not let it happen again.

When you get ready to straighten out let me know and maybe we can pick up where we left off, but for the present I am fed up with your foolishness.

Your friend,
Fred Rose

March 27, 1948

Mrs. Lillian Williams
Montgomery, Alabama

Dear Mrs. Williams,

Will you please have Hank sign the enclosed receipt for the money wired to you this morning. The contracts we spoke about on the phone were sent to Hank somewhere on Gadson Street, Pensacola, Florida. When he first arrived in Pensacola, he was in some friend's apartment. The contracts have never been returned by the Post Office so have Hank try to trace [them]. The reason I am asking Hank to sign this particular type of contract is for his own protection so he won't get too full of firewater and sign a bad contract with someone else and regret it. I hope Hank has come to his senses by now and realizes that drinking never gets people out of trouble, it only gets them in deeper.

Yours very truly,
Fred Rose

Both Hank and Audrey were chronic overspenders, and the payment they got for selling their house immediately disappeared on clothes and jewelry.

That spring, Audrey told Hank that she was divorcing him. Their house on Stuart Avenue was sold on April 3.

Fred Rose, meanwhile, was under the misapprehension that Hank had cleaned up his act.

April 3, 1948

Dear Hank,

I hear you have been doing a pretty good job of straightening yourself out and nobody is more glad to hear it than me. Hank, anything I've written you or said is for your own good as I know what a fool a man can make of himself with drinking....

You are destined for big things in the recording and songwriting field, and you are the only one who can ruin this opportunity. In the future, forget the firewater and let me take care of your business and you'll be a big name in this business.

Remember that women are revengeful and do all in their power to wreck a man when they separate from him and the only way to win is for the man to become successful.

Kind personal regards, I am...Your Friend,

Fred Rose

Prison of Memories

I

My heart nars nothing but strife
no sunshine do I euer I see
for I ~~am~~ must stay all my life
~~serving life~~
In a prison of memories

II

My prison In not made of stone
But I can ~~know all~~ ~~Be~~ neuer go free
the past is the ~~warden~~ guard with the key
~~+ guard~~
In my prison of memories

III

This world holds nothing grife

for me life just means pain
my Dungeon is deeper the sea
and know Ill never eascape
frome my prison of memories

~~This life holds nothing grife~~

My life is lived in the past
tomorrow mean nothing ~~for~~ to me
~~just~~
get another day to cry ——— regit
In my prison of memories

no key can open the door
their is no fredom for me
~~Death is the only eascape~~
frome my prison of memories

for years Ive tried to eascape

~~Ive pray~~
Ive prayed for fredom and death
frome this prison of memories

memories of days long gone by
sweet moments ~~of that~~ ~~use to be~~ yesterday
thats all the company I have
In my prison of memories

Hank's last Montgomery band. L-R:
Lum York, Red Todd, Audrey, Hank,
Joe Pennington, R. D. "Sonny" Norred

From Hank's notebook:
"You Know That I Know"

On April 8, a Grand Ole Opry touring package came to Montgomery, headlined by Johnny Bond and Cowboy Copas. As so often in the past, Hank was the local added attraction—and as so often happened, his drinking lost him a gig.

"They brought in an Opry show with Cowboy Copas, Johnny Bond, and a bunch of others. Hank was gonna bring them back to the club after the show, and Johnny come in, sang a song, we backed him up. We said, 'Is Hank with y'all?' One of them said, 'Well, the last we saw him, him and Copas was backstage with a couple of women and a bottle.' 'Well, you needn't look for him for awhile,' R.D. said [Hank's steel guitarist, R. D. Norred]. Took about three or four days before Hank ever showed up. He never shaved since before he was on that show. Found out later he'd been laid up in the hotel with one of them women. He ordered some whiskey up and they kept on bringing it. The night he showed up again, he sung a few, didn't sound too good. He talked to the bartender—who was the owner—to try and smooth things over, but then he took off, and then he never come back. Then the owner said he wasn't gonna keep paying Hank, but he'd pay us if we kept the job. We got anxious. Now, who's gonna tell Hank? Red [Todd] was scared to death. They decided I was gonna do it. Me and Red went up there. This was at a sanatorium somewhere. Hank was propped up in bed. They knew where to take him. Hank said, 'How you fellas doing? What's happening down at the club?' I said, 'Well, the owner's fixing to get another band.' Hank said, 'Oh.' I said, 'Well, he's offered us the job, and we thought we'd go ahead and take it.' He said, 'Well, do what you want.' He got kinda surly." *(Hank's band member Joe Pennington, June 2, 1992)*

On April 28, Audrey filed for divorce, stating, "Hank Williams my husband is twenty-four years of age. He has a violent and ungovernable temper. He drinks a great deal, and during the last month, he has been drunk most of the time. My nervous system has been upset and I am afraid to live with him any longer."

I

You know that I know that you ain't so good
you wouldn't Tell the True if you coued
leeing is a habit you practic were ever you go
you may fool the rest of this wored but you know that I know.

II

The last time I saw you your hair was red
but today I see you got blone hair on your head
you say youre got you an old man with pleanty dol
baby you may foole him but you know that I know

III

so baby when you pass me don't give me the run around
Cause if youll rember Im the guy that brough you to town
to some folks gale you may be mrs so & so
but don't turn your nose up at me Cause you know that I know

IV

you toled some of my friends that you turned me down
but I wouedn't have you if you were the last gal in town
if I had wonted you I coued have got you lonago
you may foole the rest of this wored but you know that I know

9/18/48

I ~~was~~ stood beside a Deep cold grave
one dark & rainy day
and watched ~~so~~ heples as its laid
my own dear darling away

I cried & prayed To God above
not to take her frome my side
But today I saw her take
That last long lonesome ride

I can't go on no use to try
I wish that I could die
I am dead and yet I live
ah God what misery.

~~I~~ I saw the heavens all turn black
I heard the winds they cried
they seemed to wisper in my ear
she taking that last long ride

On May 26, 1948, Hank and Audrey's divorce was final, but by then their always-tempestuous relationship had changed course once again and they reconciled. Hank had pulled himself back from the brink and sobered up. For the first time in Acuff-Rose's history, Fred Rose placed Hank on a retainer of fifty dollars a month. Rose also helped Hank get out of Montgomery. A new radio jamboree, the Louisiana Hayride, had just started on radio station KWKH in Shreveport. One of Rose's former songwriting partners, Dean Upson, was KWKH's commercial manager, and Rose called in a few favors to get Hank on the station.

Daily's Record Ranch, July 31, 1948. Smiling Jerry Jericho, Ben Christian, and Hank, with KNUZ deejay Biff Collie.

On Thursday, July 29, 1948, Hank Williams signed off WSFA, Montgomery, for the last time. He was on his way to Shreveport, Louisiana. Traveling first to Houston, he called on Pappy Daily, owner of Daily's Record Ranch and the area's largest record distributor, South Coast Amusements. Daily invited Hank to make some in-store appearances that Saturday.

"We started the Louisiana Hayride on KWKH, Shreveport, in April of 1948. I was the producer. I went up and watched the Grand Ole Opry, and I decided I would run it absolutely differently. With the Opry, they'd bring a guy on and you'd have to suffer through him for a half-hour whether you liked him or not. He'd bring on some guests, but essentially you had the same guy, like, say, Roy Acuff for a half-hour. If you liked him, it was great; if you didn't, it wasn't. My idea was to put the artists in extreme competition with each other. If they were going to be stars, they had to establish themselves and then reestablish themselves every Saturday night. When one of my artists came on stage, he did two numbers. If he encored, he came back later and did another two numbers, and that was all for the evening. It forced the artists to reestablish their eminence; it was a terribly difficult show to work, but it created more stars than all the other jubilee-type shows combined. More than the Grand Ole Opry, because the Opry never made stars—they go there after they're established. It's not hard to recognize a person's eminence when they're nationally known; it's darn hard to do it when no one's heard of them. The Opry referred to the Louisiana Hayride as the Grand Ole Opry farm club.

"Hank drove into Shreveport in an old Chrysler. He had his mattress and springs on top, and Audrey and her daughter by a former marriage were in there. He walked into my office, sat down and said, 'I'm Hank Williams,' and I scheduled him for that Saturday."
(Horace Logan, Louisiana Hayride program director, December 14, 1991)

(above, left) Hank is welcomed to KWKH's Louisiana Hayride by station manager Henry Clay.

(above, right) Louisiana Hayride cast shot

(right) Playing Jerry Irby's nightclub in Houston

With Fiddlin' Arthur Smith (center) and honky-tonk star Al Dexter, the originator of "Pistol Packin' Mama." Hank is wearing a suit he bought from Shreveport booking agent and artist manager Tillman Franks: "Before I was bookin', I was in a band with Claude King and Buddy Attaway. A car dealer bought us all white suits. I had it tailored for Hank by Mrs. Maxie Goldberg, who had a tailoring place across from KWKH. I sold it to Hank for sixty dollars, but he never did pay me."

Hank had been country music's brightest star in and around Montgomery, but the scene was far more localized in the 1940s, meaning that Shreveport was almost a new start. Unlike WSFA, though, KWKH broadcast on a 50,000-watt clear channel, blanketing most of the South and Southwest. When Hank appeared on KWKH's Louisiana Hayride every Saturday night, his voice was heard by millions. He had brought some musicians to Shreveport, but lack of bookings forced him to let them go almost immediately. Just a few months later, though, Hank had established himself and was sufficiently popular to recruit another band. Meanwhile, he was making a determined effort to stay sober, feeling that the pieces would finally fall into place if he could prove his reliability.

Hank with Texas honky-tonk stars Floyd Tillman and Jerry Irby. Tillman wrote classics like "It Makes No Difference Now" and "Slippin' Around," and his confessional songwriting style quite possibly gave Hank the inspiration to look within. Irby wrote one of the great Texas beerhall classics, "Drivin' Nails in My Coffin," popularized by Ernest Tubb.

(above) Hank's Shreveport band (L-R): Felton Pruett (steel guitar), Clent Holmes (guitar), Hank, possibly Red Todd (guitar), Lum York (bass)

(left) Two up-and-coming Hanks, Thompson and Williams, with KNUZ deejay Biff Collie (center)

(far left) With fellow MGM recording artist Jerry Irby at Irby's Texas Corral nightclub, Houston, 1948

"We were playing mostly high school auditoriums. We'd book for 70:30; the band would get 70 percent and the school would get 30 percent. Hank was making good money. He was paying us fifty dollars a week each. I remember one night I was wanting to talk to him about something and I was standing there while he and the principal was countin' out the money, and they counted out eight hundred dollars. We'd played two shows that night, but eight hundred dollars. Man! One time we were in Lake Charles. Hank was drinking all the way down. We poured him out, and he always wanted to play the fiddle when he was drunk. He got out there and he played 'Sally Goodin' for five minutes. We kept sayin', 'That'll do, Hank, that'll do.' He'd say, 'Naw, naw, them people just eatin' it up.' They were, too. We sold pictures during the intermission, and we sold ninety-seven dollars worth of pictures that night at ten cents a piece. We gave him the money two or three days later when he'd sobered up, and he never did know where it had come from. They loved him down there. Drunk or sober, it didn't matter. Funny thing was, his time was right on. If you could get him out there and prop him up, he'd do the show." *(Hank's steel guitarist Felton Pruett, June 8, 1992)*

The key to Hank's success in Shreveport was a 1922 pop song, "Lovesick Blues." **He'd learned it from country singer Rex Griffin, who molded it into a country song and recorded it in 1939. Although it was more complex than most of his songs, Hank had sung "Lovesick Blues" in Montgomery and, early in 1949, decided to reintroduce it to his act. Flawed as it was, there was something strangely compelling about "Lovesick Blues": the yodels, the brisk tempo, the passion Hank brought to it. Quickly, it became his showstopper.**

"The first time Hank did 'Lovesick Blues' on the Hayride, he didn't have a band. I was on the bass. We were rehearsing at KWKH and Hank was singing it in F. Then there was this part where it went from F to B-minor or something like that, and I said, 'Hank, that one chord you got in there, I can't figure it out.' He says, 'Don't worry 'bout it, hoss, just stomp your foot and grin.'" *(Tillman Franks, July 11–12, 1990)*

In January 1948, seven months before Hank left for Shreveport, the American Federation of Musicians had called a recording ban, striking for higher pension fund contributions. The record companies decided not to capitulate, and the strike lasted throughout the year. Several artists tried to circumvent the ban by recording a cappella with vocal groups, but Hank, like most performers, did not record at all from late 1947 until the strike ended in December 1948. By then, MGM had very few Hank Williams recordings left in its vault, and Fred Rose scheduled a session for December 22. During the ban, several of Rose's favorite Nashville area musicians had relocated to radio station WLW in Cincinnati, depleting the already small pool of Nashville session musicians. Rose decided to hold the session in Cincinnati so that he could use steel guitarist Jerry Byrd, electric guitarist Zeke Turner, and fiddle player Tommy Jackson. Hank recorded "There'll Be No Teardrops Tonight" and, over Rose's objections, "Lovesick Blues."

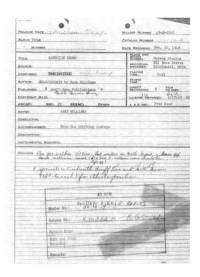

MGM Records, the session sheet for "Lovesick Blues." Note that Rex Griffin's name has been scored off the composer credit, replaced by the correct composers, Irving Mills and Cliff Friend.

"We had ten minutes left [on the session], and Hank said he had 'Lovesick Blues' in his guitar case. It was all out-of-meter, and Fred said, 'That's the worst damn thing I ever heard.' He had eyes that went different ways—he couldn't look at you with both eyes—but he was starin' hard at Hank. He said, 'I'm going down to get a cup of coffee. You can cut it if you like.' We made two cuts. I said to Hank, 'That's the sorriest thing I ever heard.' He said, 'Well, maybe we'll put it on a flip side or something.' We couldn't believe something as sorry as that [became] a hit the way it did." *(Steel guitarist Jerry Byrd, May 24, 1992)*

On May 7, 1949, "Lovesick Blues" became the number-one country record; it eventually became the best-selling country record of the year.

L-R: Hank in Cincinnati with George Blake, steel guitarist Don Davis, singer Jimmie Osborne, deejay Nelson King, and Irwin King. To ensure airplay for his new recordings, Hank had given half the composer credit on "Teardrops" to the Cincinnati-based Nelson King, who hosted a very popular late night show, Hillbilly Jamboree, on another powerful 50,000-watt station, WCKY.

"Hank was number one on the *Billboard* charts when he was still here in Shreveport. He was eating at Murrell's Grill. I bought a *Billboard* at the newsstand and walked in and showed it to him. It shook him up pretty good. He realized what that was. He hit so big and so fast." *(Tillman Franks, July 11–12, 1990)*

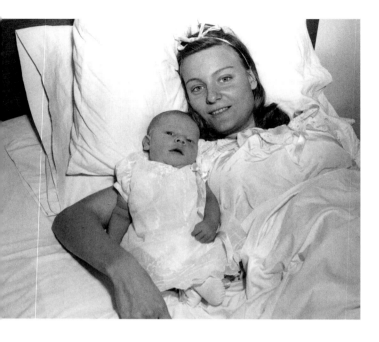

Audrey had become pregnant within days of arriving in Shreveport. Randall Hank Williams, Jr. was born on May 26, 1949, just as "Lovesick Blues" was peaking.

"Hank was thrilled to death when I became pregnant. I knew it was going to be a boy....Hank Jr. weighed ten pounds and two ounces—practically killed the both of us. It was a really bad scene for Hank. They couldn't get him away from the door. He heard me screaming. Then they told him he had a big healthy son. He was so happy, I can't tell you how happy he was. He felt so proud. Hank Jr. was so much larger than the other babies. He'd point him out to everyone." *(Audrey Williams on* Hank Williams...Reflections by Those Who Loved Him, *MGM Records, 1975)*

Finally Hank was successful enough that the Grand Ole Opry could not ignore him. **Before leaving Montgomery, Hank had met promoter Oscar Davis. He now called upon Davis to help him get to Nashville.**

"Hank called me. 'I do this number, Oscar, so help me God, I get fourteen, fifteen encores. I want to play it for you.' He played me 'Lovesick Blues.' In my mind, I said, 'This is the most horrible goddamn thing I ever heard.' He said, 'If you get me on the Opry, I'll give you twenty-five percent for life.' I said, 'You don't have to do that, but we'll get you on some way.' I came to [Opry Artist Service Bureau manager] Jim Denny, and Jim said, 'He's got a bad reputation with drinking and missing shows. There's no way we'd have him.' I pled with him and pled with him, and finally he agreed to square it away. He said, 'We'll take a chance on him.'" (Oscar Davis: Country Music Hall of Fame Oral History Project, *July 24, 1974)*

Fred Rose probably played a role in getting Hank on the Opry, too. He sweetened the pot by giving the composer credit on a song he'd written, "Chattanoogie Shoe-Shine Boy," to Opry manager Harry Stone and program director Jack Stapp. The following year, it became a number-one country hit.

Rankin File

Happy Hank's New Hits;
World's 'Toughest'

By Allen Rankin

THEY lined up three deep in front of the Charles Theater last night; they pushed and packed in to see Hank Williams, the hometown boy who has made good.

There's a Williams' smash-hit dog-house blues tune that goes:

"Move it on over,
Move it on over,
Jus' move it on over, little dog,
'Cause the big dog's movin' in."

But today, it's no little dog that's movin' it on over Hank, but the bigtime.

The Georgiana boy who plunked and sang his way to national recognition here on Station WSFA, is along with Roy Acuff and Ernest Tubbs, a star on Nashville's "Grand Old Opry," the biggest folk show in America.

Handsome Hank is not cursed by any nauseous modesty; like most real showman he's only too glad to tell you Hank isn't letting any moss grow under his feet. Right now he's as happy as we are to announce:

"I finally got one on the top—'The Lovesick Blues.' It's the Number One hit blues tune in American today—the most-played and the best-selling! . . . And another one, 'Wedding Bells,' is up in the top five.

"In other words," says Hank, "I got two of 'em up there now even bigger'n 'Move It On Over' was.

'You Pull That Sigh Out'

It doubly delighted the Showman that his old gang of Montgomery backers had turned out in such force to welcome him at his one-day personal appearance here.

"I played to three packed houses already," he told me, "and when I left just now to see my mother before the last performance, the street outside the Charles was already full. The manager says it's the biggest he's ever done with a stage show."

I asked Hank how "Love Sick Blues," the nation's top hillbilly hit goes and if I might quote a few lines. He said sure and recited:

"I got a feelin' called the blues, Oh Lawd,
Since my baby said goodbye—
Lawd, I don't know what I'll do.
All I do is set and sigh."

"You pull that last sigh out," he added, and yodelled over the phone. "Sigh-eye . . . See?"

But when I asked him what such a top hit would bring, he ducked.

"Let's don't quote no money figures," he said. "Last time you wrote me up, a government man nailed me one week from the day. He had a copy of your story in his briefcase."

"What did you tell him?"

"I told him," said Hank, "these story writers is like these hillbillies. They stretch the truth sometimes."

The author of "Lovesick Blues" is happily married and wants everyone to know he just got a "new addition," a son.

Fred Rose employed several songpluggers to tour the South, promoting Acuff-Rose songs to radio performers. Early in 1949, Acuff-Rose songplugger Mel Foree visited Hank in Shreveport and posed with him in front of Hank's new Packard touring sedan.

"Hank made his farewell appearance on the Hayride on June 3, 1949, before a standing-room-only crowd of thirty-eight hundred. Many people in the audience knew they were about to witness the end of an era. For many of them, this would be their last chance to see Hank in person….I didn't think they would ever let him stop singing 'Lovesick Blues' that night….They called Hank back for encore after encore, seven of them in all. 'Thank you,' he said when the din finally died down enough. 'I want to thank y'all from the bottom of my heart, and I'm making you a promise right now. One of these days, I'll be back.'" (*Horace Logan* in Elvis, Hank & Me, *St. Martin's Press, New York, NY, 1998*)

"Hank was on last. People were hollering for him. Horace Logan introduced him. Horace always wore guns and a cowboy hat, and worked out of a little three-sided booth. Hank came on at 10:30. Skinny as a rail. He had some telegrams. Cocked his hat back. He read out a request from a sergeant and his wife at Barksdale Air Force base. He'd read a request, then toss it away, then another one and toss it away. I thought, 'God, man, is this cool or what?' Then he said, 'Let her go, boys.' He did nothing but 'Lovesick Blues' until sign-off."
(*Mitchell Torok, February 1996*)

"Hank went off to join an Opry tour. He said, 'I'm goin' to Texas tomorrow. If I call you, you have a job. If I don't, you don't.' He didn't call." (*Hank's guitarist Bob McNett, 1991*)

5 "HILLBILLY HITS THE JACKPOT": NASHVILLE, 1949-1951

In June 1949, Hank moved to Nashville and quickly became country music's biggest star. He soon eclipsed his heroes, Roy Acuff and Ernest Tubb. His only serious rivals were smoother-voiced singers like Eddy Arnold and Red Foley, who were closer to pop than country. Hank, though, remained unapologetically hillbilly and, unlike most of his contemporaries, wrote most of his songs. After breaking onto the Grand Ole Opry with two non-originals, "Lovesick Blues" and "Wedding Bells," he took a stand with self-composed songs, such as "Mind Your Own Business," "You're Gonna Change or I'm Gonna Leave," "Long Gone Lonesome Blues," "Moanin' the Blues," "Cold, Cold Heart," and "I Can't Help It (If I'm Still in Love with You)." Their success encouraged him to work harder still at his songwriting.

Hillbilly Hits the Jackpot
After Lean Years in Youth

By WOOD SOANES

Sometime during the course of the "Grand Ole Opry" show at the Auditorium tonight a young man with sad brown eyes and sunken cheeks will arise and sing his own composition "Long Gone Lonesome Blues."

His name is Hank Williams and you probably never heard of him or his "Long Gone Lonesome Blues," but I have it on the best authority that the number leads the hillbilly hit parade and that Williams is doing very well by himself in a financial way.

Not only is the "Grand Ole Opry" a phenomenal show but the people who make it up are on the extraordinary side. Take this Williams fellow, for ex-

MacArthur and Ben Hecht to go to work on an adaptation of Sardou's "Fedora" . . . "Lost in the Stars" has ended its Broadway engagement and started on tour.

HOLLYWOOD HIGHLIGHTS

Ben Hecht will take his first

Hank was now sober for months at a time, so his domestic life was blighted only by ceaseless travel. Grand Ole Opry performers were expected to be on hand for the Saturday night show. Afterward, they would often leave to work a country music park in Pennsylvania, Ohio, or Virginia, then play clubs and theaters the rest of the week before racing back to Nashville the next Saturday. Hank spent the weeks away from Audrey, Lycrecia, and Hank Jr., and it was only on weekends, when he returned for the Opry, that they could they be together as a family.

"We kept horses out back, Hank, Lycrecia, and me. When Hank Jr. was about two years old, Hank and I were visiting Senator LeBlanc in Louisiana and he wanted to give Hank Jr. a little Shetland pony. They crated him up, put him in the back of the limousine, and brought him back to Nashville." (*Audrey Williams, 1971*)

Hank and Hank Jr., 1950

Acuff-Rose PUBLICATIONS
NASHVILLE, TENNESSEE
STATEMENT OF ROYALTIES
January 1, 1950 TO June 30, 1950

FOR HANK WILLIAMS

COMPOSITION	NO. OF COPIES SOLD	RE-TURNED COPIES	RATE	MECH.	FOREIGN	RATE	TOTAL ROYALTY
				CARRIED	OVER $		6775.35
							-4.20
YOU'RE GONNA CHANGE	289	429	.03	$ 427.88		50%	213.94
MGM				5.90		50%	2.95
Compo Ltd.				19.96		50%	9.98
Charlton-lyric				1.88		50%	.94
WMC Trans.				283.94		50%	141.97
BMI Perf.							
HANK WILLIAMS COUNTRY FOLIO	7300	—	.06				438.00
HOUSE OF GOLD	—	—	—				72.95
Coral				145.91		50%	
THE ALABAMA WALTZ	300	—	.03				9.00
CALLING YOU	—	—	—				
MGM				76.68		50%	38.34
Charlton-lyric				3.33		50%	1.66
BMI Perf.				4.24		50%	2.12
JESUS REMEMBERED ME	—	—	—				
Naughton Trans.				25.00		50%	12.50
							9.69
MY SON CALLS ANOTHER DADDY	646	—	.01½				369.39
MGM				1477.59		25%	
Charlton-lyric				10.00		25%	2.50
ROCKIN' CHAIR DADDY	—	—	—				
MGM				43.50		25%	10.88
WEALTH WON'T SAVE YOUR SOUL	—	—	—				
Naughton Trans.				25.00		50%	12.50
WHY DON'T YOU LOVE ME	—	—	—				
Charlton-lyric				3.33		50%	1.67
					TOTAL EARNINGS		8122.13
				LESS OUTSTANDING ADVANCES			6381.97
				NET DUE	$		1740.16

ACUFF-ROSE PUBLICATIONS
PER Fred Rose

FORM NO. 1051   ROYALTY EARNINGS STATEMENT

M G M RECORDS
DIVISION OF
LOEW'S INC.
120 ARLINGTON AVE. BLOOMFIELD, N. J.

No. 2415

PERIOD ENDING 2 28 50

HANK WILLIAMS

TITLE	RECORD NUMBER	SIDE	QUANTITY	UNIT ROYALTY	AMOUNT
MOVE IT ON OVER	1 0 0 3 3	A	5 8 8 6	01 0 0 0	58 86
HEARD YOU CRY O YOUR SLEEP	1 0 0 3 3	B	5 8 8 6	01 0 0 0	58 86
ROOTIE TOOTIE	1 0 1 2 4	A	1 4 4 0	01 0 0 0	14 40
SWEET LOVE AINT AROUND	1 0 1 2 4	B	1 4 4 0	01 0 0 0	14 40
I'LL BE A BACHELOR	1 0 1 7 1	A	4 5 2 3	01 0 0 0	45 23
HONKY TONKIN	1 0 1 7 1	B	4 5 2 3	01 0 0 0	45 23
I'M A LONG GONE DADDY	1 0 2 1 2	A	4 6 3 3	01 0 0 0	46 33
THE BLUES COME AROUND	1 0 2 1 2	B	4 6 3 3	01 0 0 0	46 33
PAN AMERICAN	1 0 2 2 6	A	3 9 5 5	01 0 0 0	39 55
I DON'T CARE	1 0 2 2 6	B	3 9 5 2	01 0 0 0	39 55
I SAW LIGHT	1 0 2 7 1	A	2 5 4 2	01 0 0 0	25 42
SIX MORE MILES	1 0 2 7 1	B	2 5 4 2	01 0 0 0	25 42
MANSION ON THE HILL	1 0 3 2 8	A	1 6 3 7 5	01 0 0 0	163 75
I CANT GET YOU OFF MY MIND	1 0 3 2 8	B	1 6 3 7 5	01 0 0 0	163 75
LOVESICK BLUES	1 0 3 5 2	A	1 4 8 2 4 2	01 0 0 0	1 482 42
NEVER AGAIN	1 0 3 5 2	B	1 4 8 2 4 2	01 0 0 0	1 482 42
WEDDING BELLS	1 0 4 0 1	A	8 1 8 1 3	01 0 0 0	818 13
IVE JUST TOLD MAMA GOODBYE	1 0 4 0 1	B	8 1 8 1 3	01 0 0 0	818 13
DEAR BROTHER	1 0 4 3 4	A	7 3 9	01 0 0 0	7 39
LOST ON THE RIVER	1 0 4 3 4	B	7 3 9	01 0 0 0	7 39
MIND YOUR OWN BUSINESS	1 0 4 6 1	A	3 0 9 0 1	01 0 0 0	309 01
NO TEAR DROPS TONIGHT	1 0 4 6 1	B	3 0 9 0 1	01 0 0 0	309 01
YOU'RE GONNA CHANGE	1 0 5 0 6	A	1 0 8 2 1 7	01 0 0 0	1 082 17
LOST HIGHWAY	1 0 5 0 6	B	1 0 8 2 1 7	01 0 0 0	1 082 17
MY BUCKETS GOT A HOLE	1 0 5 6 0	A	1 1 4 6 2 4	01 0 0 0	1 146 24
I'M LONESOME I COULD CRY	1 0 5 6 0	B	1 1 4 6 2 4	01 0 0 0	1 146 24

Acuff-Rose PUBLICATIONS
NASHVILLE, TENNESSEE
STATEMENT OF ROYALTIES
January 1, 1950 TO June 30, 1950

FOR HANK WILLIAMS

COMPOSITION	NO. OF COPIES SOLD	RE-TURNED COPIES	RATE	MECH.	FOREIGN	RATE	TOTAL ROYALTY
				CARRIED	OVER $		1684.83
I JUST DON'T LIKE LIVING	1099	63	.03				31.08
MGM				1272.25		50%	636.12
Charlton-lyric				10.00		50%	5.00
Mutual Trans.				7.50		50%	3.75
I'M SO LONESOME I COULD CRY	1202	149	.03				31.59
MGM				1476.99		50%	738.49
Compo Ltd.				26.24		50%	13.12
Decca				256.14		50%	128.07
BMI Perf.				98.92		50%	49.46
LONG GONE LONESOME BLUES	2860	—	.03				85.80
Four Star				3.21		50%	1.60
MGM				1477.59		50%	738.79
Charlton-lyric				10.00		50%	5.00
MANSION ON THE HILL	535	301	.01½				3.51
MGM				179.33		25%	44.83
Charlton-lyric				5.00		25%	1.25
Naughton Trans.				25.00		25%	6.25
Mutual Trans.				7.50		25%	1.87
MIND YOUR OWN BUSINESS	104	867	.03				-22.89
Vocalion				5.43		50%	2.71
Victor				176.03		50%	88.01
Victor Ltd.				55.90		50%	27.95
Decca				74.25		50%	37.12
MGM				233.97		50%	116.99
Charlton-lyric				12.33		50%	6.16
WMC Trans.				1.87		50%	.94
Naughton Trans.				25.00		50%	12.50
BMI Perf.				703.60		50%	351.80
MAY YOU NEVER BE ALONE	554	17	.03				16.11
MGM				1272.25		50%	636.12
				CARRIED	OVER		5483.93

ACUFF-ROSE PUBLICATIONS
Fred Rose

The money flowed in, and in September 1949, Hank and
Audrey bought a house on Franklin Road, Nashville.
All new furniture, new cars, and horses followed.

"Homesick"

I

Homesick and lonely, worried and blue
Wants see the baby and the baby's mama to
so tired groaning bout to lose my mind
Homesick and lonesome for that gal of mind

II

Mean old trouble is all that I've known
I'm missing my honey Boy I'm going home
If she'll just let me tarry when I come draging in
you couldn't take a shotgut and run me off again

III

This old boy's got misery in his soul
This old worried to big and to cold
I'm riding that freight train when she comes down the tracks
and next time you see me leaving I'll be flat of my back

IV

I never new a body could feel so low
I keep asking my self why did you ever go
I'm heading home and there I'm gona park
and if she wants it that way I'm gona learn how to Bark

Feb 8th
1951
Hank Williams

Audrey was still a part of Hank's show in the early Nashville days. Here they're shown with two fans. Don Helms and Sammy Pruett look on from the wings.

Even the weekends were sometimes full of commitments. Hank would prerecord shows for several sponsors, Mother's Best Flour and Duck Head Overalls among them.

Two fans have just bought one of Hank's song folios and pose alongside Hank, Don Helms, and Bob McNett.

Shortly after settling in Nashville, Hank recruited a new band. He called steel guitarist Don Helms, who had worked with him in Montgomery, and guitarist Bob McNett, who had worked with him in Shreveport. He recruited a young fiddle player, Jerry Rivers, and bassist Hillous Butrum. The Opry assigned him an opening act, Big Bill Lister. McNett left in 1950 to be replaced by Sammy Pruett, who had also worked with Hank in Montgomery, and Butrum was replaced by Howard Watts, who did on-stage comedy as "Cedric Rainwater."

"Hank had called me from Shreveport. He had needed a fiddler on the Hayride. He offered me fifty dollars a week, and that was a pretty decent salary, but that's what I was making here [in Nashville] and I didn't want to move. The following year, 'Lovesick Blues' hit, and the next thing I knew I read in the paper that Hank had signed with the Grand Ole Opry and was moving to Nashville. This upset me 'cause by now it was a prestige move to go with him. Then a friend of mine [Jack Boles] came by and said that Hank was putting together a band and said I should go ask him for a job. Jack took me over there and said to Hank, 'This is Jerry Rivers. He wants to talk to you about a job.' I had my fiddle in my hand, and as soon as I opened the case up he reached in and got it hisself. He plunked on it and sawed on it. He said, 'Can you play "Sally Goodin"?' Could I play 'Sally Goodin'! He was stompin' that foot, flailin' on the guitar. We must have played it for five minutes, then he set down his guitar and I set down the fiddle, and he said, 'Well, anyone [who] can play "Sally Goodin" better'n me is a pretty good fiddle player. You're hired.' We worked for fifteen dollars a day, which was five dollars a day over scale. Then we made more money selling Hank Williams songbooks. Sometimes we'd sell as many as one thousand songbooks a night." *(Jerry Rivers, undated interview)*

Hank was by far the most charismatic act in
country music, holding an audience riveted
from the moment he stepped on stage.

Hank's passport photo

L-R: Minnie Pearl, Little Jimmy Dickens (squatting), Roy Acuff, Hank surrounded by two local children, Opry comedian Rod Brasfield (standing), and host of the Prince Albert Opry, Red Foley (squatting).

Hank and Red Foley disembarking in Vienna

With Roy Acuff's daughter, Thelma, a dancer on the Opry show

EUROPE: NOVEMBER 1949

The only time Hank went overseas was on a Grand Ole Opry tour of American forces bases in Europe in November 1949. A relative newcomer to the Opry, he couldn't bring his own band, but because the cast would be away over Thanksgiving, he and the other cast members were allowed to bring their spouses.

"We flew in what had been General Eisenhower's plane. We stopped in Newfoundland, Canada, on the way over. God, I'd never been so cold. Didn't play there, just refueled, then went on to Paris, stopped a short while, then flew on to Weisbaden in Germany. Hank was stone cold sober every day. They issued us orders in Russian just in case we got lost and wandered into the Russian sector. Hank looked at this sheet of writing in Russian and said, 'Hell, they ain't never gonna win the next war. They cain't even spell.' On the way back, we stopped in Bermuda to refuel. Coming in, we hit an air pocket. A couple of guys were literally flying through the airplane. We'd bought cuckoo clocks somewhere in the Black Forest and all these clocks were falling out into the aisle and makin' cuckoo noises. We didn't stay long in Bermuda. Just a few hours, maybe overnight. It was a British colony and we'd never seen anybody drive on the wrong side of the road before." *(Red Foley's steel guitarist, Billy Robinson, March 5, 2001)*

"It was one of the greatest experiences of my life. It was a great, great show and we worked for some wonderful military audiences. We appeared in big theaters in Berlin and all those cities. It was a little depressing to see those beautiful cities bombed and flattened out. A city the size of Detroit laying in rubble. But they were building it back even then." *(Little Jimmy Dickens interviewed by Eddie Stubbs in* Country Boy, *Bear Family Records, 1997)*

"Hank was a terrible eater. You could take him into the finest gourmet restaurant, and he'd slop the food on his plate and say, 'Hey, Herman, bring me the ketchup.' He did that in Germany at one of the best restaurants. The maître d' said he couldn't have ketchup, and Hank like to have wrecked the joint." *(Whitey Ford, the Duke of Paducah)*

"Hank loved America. A couple of years ago, he was one of the Opry stars who flew to Europe to entertain the American servicemen, which he did beautifully. He swore that if he ever got back home, he would kiss the ground. When he got off the plane at Nashville airport, he did just that: He kneeled over slowly and kissed the ground." *(Grand Ole Opry announcer George D. Hay in a broadcast, January 10, 1953)*

(far left) Hank, Little Jimmy Dickens, and Minnie Pearl are serenaded by a service band on arrival in Germany.

(left) Flying the flag for WSM's Grand Ole Opry. Hank with Roy Acuff's accordionist, Jimmy Riddle, and Red Foley's bassist, Joe Zinkan. Steel guitarist Billy Robinson is just visible behind Hank.

Thanksgiving away from home. Hank and Audrey with Little Jimmy Dickens and Minnie Pearl

Hank and Roy Acuff with Helen Bremer and an unidentified soldier

Stopping over in Bermuda on the way back to Nashville

The Drifting Cowboys and Hank's fellow performers were in awe of his ability to mesmerize an audience.

"I could not then, nor can I yet understand the almost uncanny power Hank Williams held over his audience. As we rolled out of Nashville in Hank's long, blue Packard after [my] first Opry appearance [with Hank], I sat quietly in the back knowing I had changed. In those few moments on stage at the Opry, watching Hank perform and watching the audience respond, I regained a humility I'd lost somewhere along the way." *(Jerry Rivers, From Life to Legend, Heather Publications, Denver, CO, 1967)*

"He had a charisma about him when he got on stage. He could get a crowd of people in the palm of his hand and just wring 'em out. I've often said that once Hank walked out there with that ol' guitar and curled up around that mic, a naked lady coulda rode an African elephant behind him and wouldn't nobody have seen her. That's how he could captivate an audience. The show depended on the mood. You had to watch for him. He might walk out and start with a fast or slow one. It wasn't automatic pilot with him. He was so popular and so hot, I often wondered why they hired me to warm the crowd up—they didn't need no warming." *(Hank's supporting act, Big Bill Lister, June 1992)*

A Sunday showdate in a country music park. Hank is with Jerry Rivers, Sammy Pruett, and Cedric Rainwater. The parks often paid as much as one thousand dollars for a day's work, and Hank was one of the best draws on the circuit.

Contract Blank

AMERICAN FEDERATION OF MUSICIANS

Local Number_____

THIS CONTRACT for the personal services of musicians, made this __22nd__ day of __MARCH__ 19_51_
between the undersigned employer (hereinafter called the employer) and __FIVE__ musicians' (hereinafter called employees) represented by the undersigned representative.

(including Leaders)

WITNESSETH, That the employer employs the personal services of the employees, as musicians severally, and the employees severally, through their representative, agree to render collectively to the employer services as musicians in the orchestra under the leadership of__HANK WILLIAMS__

Name and Address of Place of Engagement __AUDITORIUM, SHREVEPORT, LA.__ according to the following terms and conditions:

Date(s) of employment __WEDNESDAY APRIL 4, 1951__

Hours of employment __8:00 to 10:00 pm__

The employer is hereby given an option to extend this agreement for a period of __no__ weeks beyond the original term thereof. Said option can be made effective only by written notice from the employer to the employees not later than _____ days prior to the expiration of said original term that he claims and exercises said option.

PRICE AGREED UPON $__Scale PRIVILEGE FIFTY PERCENT OF GROSS RECEIPTS (TAX EXCLUDED)__

(Terms and Amount)

This price includes expenses agreed to be reimbursed by the employer in accordance with the attached schedule, or a schedule to be furnished the employer on or before the date of engagement.

To be paid __AT CONCLUSION OF ENGAGEMENT__

(Specify When Payments Are to Be Made)

The employer shall at all times have complete control of the services which the employees will render under the specifications of this contract. On behalf of the employer the Leader will distribute the amount received from the employer to the employees, including himself, as indicated on the opposite side of this contract, or in place thereof on separate memorandum supplied to the employees, including himself, as ment of the employment hereunder and take and turn over to the employer receipts therefor from each employer, including himself. The amount paid to the Leader includes the cost of transportation, which will be reported by the Leader to the employer at or before the commence-the Leader on his behalf to replace any employee who by illness, absence, or for any other reason does not perform any or all of the services provided for under this contract. The agreement of the employees to perform is subject to proven detention by sickness, accidents, or accidents by means of transportation, riots, strikes, epidemics, acts of God, or any other legitimate conditions beyond the control of the employee. The employer agrees that the Business Representative of the Musicians' Local in whose jurisdiction the musicians are playing, shall have access to the premises in which the musicians perform (except in private residences) for the purpose of conferring with the musicians. The performing services under this contract must be members of the American Federation of Musicians and nothing in this contract shall ever be construed as to interfere with any obligation which they may owe to the American Federation of Musicians, subject, however, to all applicable laws.

To the extent that their inclusion and enforcement are not prohibited by a valid federal or state statute, the rules, laws and regulations of the American Federation of Musicians, and the rules, laws and regulations of the Local in whose jurisdiction the musicians perform, insofar as they are not in conflict with those of the Federation, are made part of this contract, and to such extent nothing in this contract shall ever be construed as to interfere with any obligation which any employee hereunder may owe to the American Federation of Musicians pursuant thereto.

Any member or members who are parties to or affected by this contract, whose services thereunder are covered thereby, are prevented, suspended or stopped by reason of any strike, ban, unfair list order or requirement of the Federation or persons without any restraint, hindrance, penalty, obligation employment of the same or similar character, or otherwise, for other employers or persons without any restraint, hindrance, penalty, obligation or liability whatever, any other provisions of this contract to the contrary notwithstanding.

If this contract requires or contemplates the recording, transmission or reproduction of any music by any mechanical means, then it shall not become effective unless and until it shall have been approved by the International Executive Board of the American Federation of Musicians.

The employer represents that there does not exist against him, in favor of any employee-member of the American Federation of Musicians, any claim of any kind arising out of musical services rendered for any such employer. It is agreed that no employee-member of the American Federation of Musicians will be required to perform any provisions of this contract or to render any services for said employer as long as any such claim is unsatisfied or unpaid, in whole or in part. The employer in signing this contract himself, or having same signed by a representa-tive, acknowledges his (her or their) authority to do so and hereby assumes liability for the amount stated herein.

Name of Employer __HENRY CLAY__   Accepted by Employer _Henry Clay (MGR)_

Street Address __RADIO STATION KWKH__   Accepted _Hank Williams_

City __SHREVEPORT__ State __La.__   _(Orchestra Leader)_

Phone _____   Address _____

                                                    By _____

                                                    (Representatives of Employees)

If contracted by licensed booker, he must insert on the reverse side on contract the name, address and telephone number of the local collecting agent of the American Federation of Musicians in whose jurisdiction the engagement covered by the contract is to be played.

9-15-49   FORM B-1   Printed in U.S.A.

Almost two years after leaving the Louisiana Hayride, Hank returned to Shreveport for one appearance in April 1951. His former boss, KWKH's Henry Clay, promoted the show.

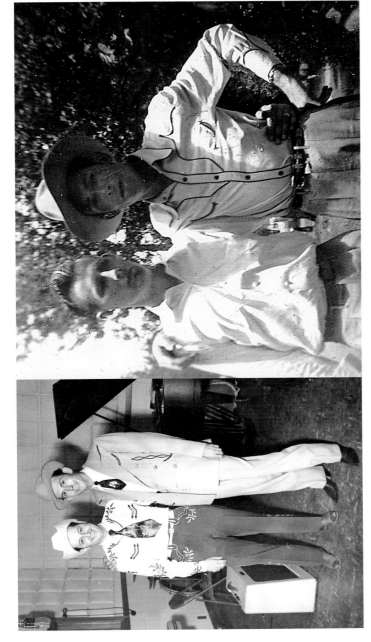

With fellow Opry star George Morgan,
father of current country star Lorrie Morgan

With western swing bandleader
Merl Lindsay, Oklahoma City

"They had put me in the closing spot 'cause at that time I was pretty wild on stage. Somewhere in Kansas, they told me Hank Williams had joined the show. They put him on before me. Oh, man! He just split 'em up. I stood there in the wings watching him mesmerize 'em, and I knew I had to follow him. I know who old Minnie Pearl can follow, and I knew I couldn't follow him. I tried to go on, and they kept on saying, 'We want Hank.' We were staying at some little ol' hotel and I waited in the lobby for Oscar Davis, and I walked over to him, and I said, 'We got another couple of nights on this tour, [and you] put [Hank] on after me. From now until the end of time, Minnie Pearl is going to go ahead of him.' I wasn't going to follow him the longest day I lived." (*Minnie Pearl on Hank Williams…Reflections by Those Who Loved Him, MGM Records, 1975*)

Contract Blank

AMERICAN FEDERATION OF MUSICIANS

Local Number..............

THIS CONTRACT for the personal services of musicians, made this 20th day of JANUARY 19 51

between the undersigned employer (hereinafter called the employer) and... musicians (including Leaders)

WITNESSETH, That the employer employs the personal services of the employees, as musicians severally, and the employees severally, through their representative, agree to render collectively to the employer services as musicians in the orchestra under the leadership of JIMMY DICKENS, according to the following terms and conditions:

Name and Address of Place of Engagement HANK WILLIAMS GRAND OLE OPRY SHOW, GYMNASIUM, COOKSVILLE (NEAR MT. PLEASANT), TEXAS

Date(s) of employment TUESDAY JANUARY 30, 1951

Hours of employment 8:00 P.M.

The employer is hereby given an option to extend this agreement for a period of... no weeks beyond the original term thereof. Said option can be made effective only by written notice from the employer to the employees not later than... days prior to the expiration of said original term that he claims and exercises said option.

PRICE AGREED UPON $ 750.00 MINIMUM 60% OF GROSS RECEIPTS (Terms and Amount)
ON COMMISSION OF ENGAGEMENT
(Specify When Payments Are to Be Made)

This price includes expenses agreed to be reimbursed by the employer in accordance with the attached schedule, or a schedule to be furnished the employer on or before the date of engagement.

Accepted by Employer...
Accepted...
Address...
By...
(Representatives of Employees)

Name of Employer WESTERN SWING ENTERPRISES, INC.

Street Address 3510 PLEASANT VALLEY ROAD

City NASHVILLE State TENN.

Phone...

If contracted by licensed booker, he must insert on the reverse side on contract the name, address and telephone number of the local collecting agent of the American Federation of Musicians in whose jurisdiction the engagement is to be played.

FORM B-1 Printed in U.S.A.
9-15-49

"The mystery of Hank Williams, I have never been able to figure out. What was the magnetism that he had? Any time you worked a concert with him, you didn't have to peek around the curtain to see if you had a full house. You knew it. It was always there and he'd tell you so. 'I drew you a full house, now go out and entertain 'em!' When he came on stage, it was over. People would come unglued." (*Little Jimmy Dickens interviewed by Eddie Stubbs for Country Boy, Bear Family Records, 1995*)

(opposite, left) One of the few remaining show contracts from Hank's career, this is for an Opry double bill of Hank and Little Jimmy Dickens. They shared $750 as an advance on 60 percent of door receipts.

(opposite, right) Hank and Little Jimmy Dickens

(above, left) After the Opry went off air, the Midnite Jamboree from the Ernest Tubb Record Shop came on. Hank guested occasionally.

(above, right) With Tubb sidemen Billy Byrd and Jack Drake

(bottom, left) Quartet with Grady Martin, Don Helms, and Billy Byrd

At the opening of Hank and Audrey's Corral, June 1951, Roy Acuff performed while Hank looked on. Gathered around Hank and Acuff (L-R) are Jerry Rivers, Cedric Rainwater on bass, Big Bill Lister on guitar, and Sammy Pruett on guitar.

In 1947 Opry star Ernest Tubb opened a record store in Nashville. Perhaps in emulation of Tubb's success with this venture, Hank and Audrey opened a western clothing business, Hank and Audrey's Corral, at 724 Commerce Street, near Tubb's store and near the Opry. Unlike Tubb's record shop, which is still in business, Hank and Audrey's Corral was a marginal concern at the best of times.

HANK

HANK & AUDREY'S
CORRAL

TELEPHONE 5-4453

724 COMMERCE ST.   •   NASHVILLE, TENN.

AUDREY

HEART FILLED WITH HATE

I

MY DARLING I KNOW HOW HARD YOU HAVE TRIED
TO SMILE AGAIN AND KEEP YOUR EYES DRIED
IT'S SAD BUT'S IT'S TRUE MY LOVE CAME TO LATE
FOR DARLING I'M WED TO A HEART FILLED WITH HATE

2

THE HATE FOR ANOTHER YOU HOLD IN YOUR HEART
WILL KILL OUR LOVE AND DRIVE US APART
IT'S BEST THAT I GO AND BLAME IT ON FATE
FOR DARLING I'M WED TO A HEART FILLED WITH HATE

3

I'VE TRIED AND I'VE TRIED TO HELP YOU FORGET
BUT I'VE FAILD CAUSE YOUR LIFE IS ONE BIG REGRETT
SO IT'S USELESS FOR ME TO HOPE AND TO WATE
FOR DARLING I'M WED TO A HEART FILLED WITH HATE

4

I CAN NEVER UNDO WHAT ANOTHER HAS DONE
SO WHEN YOU WAKE IN THE MORNING DEAR I'LL BE GONE
BUT I'LL PRAY EVERY NITE THAT YOU'LL SOON ESCAPE
FROME YOUR POOR HEART THAT'S DYING FROME HATE

ACUFF_ROSE PUBLICATIONS __ B M I

HANK WILLIAMS OCT 9 I95I

THE MONTGOMERY HOMECOMING : JULY 15, 1951

Hank Williams Accepts Montgomery's Invitation

Hank Williams, the local boy who has skyrocketed into the position of the nation's No. 1 Hillbilly singer and composer, has accepted an invitation to appear at the Cow Coliseum in Montgomery, Sunday afternoon, July 15, at 3 o'clock. The occasion will be a special "Homecoming for Hank Williams Day," sponsored by the Montgomery Jaycees. This will be the first big show

With Audrey, Hank Jr., and Lycrecia backstage at the Montgomery Homecoming

With local deejay Uncle Bob Helton

Lillie is feted by a representative of the Jaycees.

The Montgomery Jaycees offered Hank a "Homecoming." There was an afternoon show at the Veterans' Hospital and a parade, climaxing in a show at the newly built Agricultural Coliseum. Lillie was presented with a gold watch, and Hank publicly acknowledged his debt to her.

"Yes siree, let me grab a minute on my old home station. Howdee everybody. I'm just plumb tickled to be comin' home for the show at the Coliseum. I'm just as grateful as can be to the Jaycees for puttin' on this how-dee-do. Makes a fella mighty proud and puts a lump in his throat. This trip home is gonna bring on a lot of memories. I was on WSFA eleven years, nine days, and six months pickin' and singin' for you all. This show's gonna be a humdinger: all the boys and myself and Big Bill Lister, and there's gonna be such great folk music stars as Hank Snow. That boy is really kickin' up dust all over this country. Them train songs of his are as hot as a two-dollar pistol after a feud. Talkin' 'bout entertainment, just wait 'til you see the Carter Sisters with Mother Maybelle. They'll have you stompin' and clappin' 'fore you even get set down in your seats. Just like the advertisement says, this will be the biggest folk music show ever to come to Montgomery. When a boy grows up in a town and makes a little name for himself and the folks are nice enough to bring him back and designate a whole day as a homecomin', well folks just couldn't be no nicer. Some of the boys out at the veterans hospital aren't gonna be able to come to the Coliseum, so on Sunday afternoon we gonna go out there and put on a show for 'em. Until then, this is Hank Williams sayin' if the good Lord's willin' and the creeks don't rise, I'll see you July 15th." *(Hank Williams, radio promo spot for the Homecoming)*

"Somehow, Hank came back here for the Homecoming without a guitar. He and I drove down to French's Music Store on Court Square. We double-parked. He went in and I stayed in the car. Ten or fifteen minutes later, he came out with a guitar. He said, 'Ten years ago, I wanted to buy a guitar here on credit and they wouldn't sell it to me. Now they want to give me one.' He thought a lot about things like that and yearned for the old days. Back then, if someone liked him, they liked him because he was just Hank and not a star who could maybe do something for him." *(Hank's cousin Walter McNeil, February 5, 2001)*

"I sang [two songs Hank had written,] 'Rockin' Chair Daddy' and 'Teardrop on a Rose' at the Coliseum. I was sitting back there with Mother Maybelle. Hank was sitting in a chair waiting to go on the show. This li'l guy, Gene Taunton, come in. He was maybe fifteen or sixteen, he walked in with a guitar. He said, 'Hey Hank, how about letting me sing a song on the show,' and Hank said, 'Well, I'm sorry son, but I already got my program made out.' This guy said, 'All I do is sing your songs, just let me sing one song.' Hank said, 'Well, what you want to do?' This guy said, 'I want to do "Hey Good Lookin'."' Hank said, 'Well, that's my current song.' This guy said, 'Aw Hank let me sing it.' Hank said, 'Go 'head, I'll sing something else.' I don't know who else would've done that." *(Former Drifting Cowboy Braxton Schuffert, December 16, 1992)*

After the show, Hank returned to Lillie's boarding house. He took off his shirt to show everyone his new stainless steel back brace. The following morning, he set off for southern Mississippi and Louisiana.

"Shortly after the Homecoming, Hank was driving through Louisiana. Everywhere he stopped, he had a cajun fish dish called jumbalaya. The cajuns, a happy lot, would say, 'Mister Hank, have fun!' Hank went out and sat in the back of his Cadillac, where he writes many a song, and put the whole kettle o'fish together. It would have been out sooner, but his publisher didn't think it would go." *(Allen Rankin in the* Montgomery Advertiser, *September 28, 1952)*

Mother Maybelle and the Carter Sisters perform with Chet Atkins

Montgomery's Agricultural Coliseum on the day of the Homecoming

Songwriting income, record royalties, and Opry appearance fees were small change. Hank's bread-and-butter was the road. Country music fans demanded that their stars be accessible—every last autograph signed, every last hand shaken. No one was gladder than Hank to do it. He had worked all his life for this.

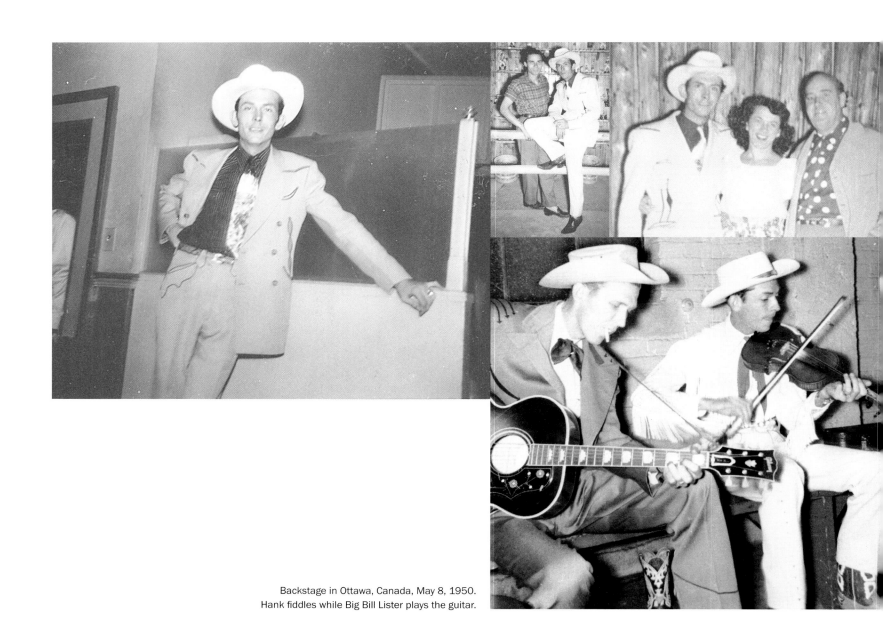

Backstage in Ottawa, Canada, May 8, 1950.
Hank fiddles while Big Bill Lister plays the guitar.

Hank with fans

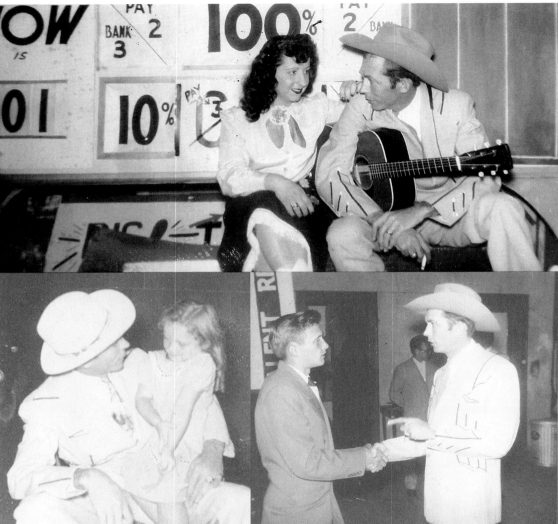

"In this business if you're a success there's some folks who actually worship you. I've been to some places where it's impossible to walk across the stage without having the major portion of my outfit torn off. They even grab fistfuls of hair. When you get to be a success, folks have a habit of writing you and telling you their troubles. All kinds of troubles. If their husband dies and they're left with eight starving kids, they write. If their sweetheart done them wrong, they write. If they feel sorta blue, they write. I dunno, I reckon they think I'm something like the Red Cross." *(Hank Williams, interviewed in Charleston, South Carolina, March 2, 1951)*

Hank in Ottawa, Canada, May 8, 1950. Here he's standing with a blind singer, Freda Blair (left), who opened his show, and with John Corrigan of radio station CFRA (above).

Guitarist Bob McNett rejoined Hank in Nashville but quit in 1950 to open a country music park, Bob and Dean's Radio Corral, in Montgomery, Pennsylvania. It had an on-site photo booth where Hank posed with Mom McNett and her friend Gay Merrick.

Backstage in Toronto, October 27, 1949, Hank chats with Eve Lyons, president of the Earl Heywood Fan Club.

The road was a terrible but necessary grind. The ceaseless travel exacerbated his back problems, which he alleviated with ever-increasing doses of painkillers and, occasionally, alcohol.

Hank and an unknown fan.

"By today's standards, traveling back then was very primitive. We drove mostly on two-lane roads, and everybody went in one car. Until Hank became a big star and could afford a limo, it was just a regular car. First a Packard, then a Fleetwood. Eventually, he got a Cadillac limo, and that eased everything a lot. We played a lot of one-nighters and often drove four or five hundred miles between towns. Without interstates or bypasses, you went right through the center of every city, and at certain times of day, they were rough to get through. To get a decent room and meal, you usually had to stay in a downtown hotel and eat at a nearby restaurant. This was before motels became popular and restaurants became available at every interstate exit. With all of his back problems, Hank rode the car in misery. But he was right there with us. Just one of the boys. It was tough, but when Hank was on his way up, we were right where we wanted to be in the music business." *(Don Helms in* The Complete Hank Williams, *Mercury Records, 1998)*

"Hank was the only person I ever saw could put ketchup on his oatmeal. Out on the road, none of us ate properly. We'd stop to get gas, and at the same time, we'd get a gallon of milk and a dozen doughnuts or cupcakes. We didn't even have time to order hamburgers a lot of the time. There were many weeks that we'd maybe check into a hotel twice—the rest of the time you're driving." *(Big Bill Lister, June 10, 1992)*

A very hot evening, just after sundown, August 27, 1950.
Hank had just appeared at Natural Chimneys Park,
Mt. Solon, Virginia.

Posing at a country music park

Searching in vain

I

I walk the lonely streets of life day after day
hopeing and praying that you will pass my way
Longing for just a glimpse of your face again
walking the road of life and searching in vain

II

Searching for a treasure that I know's forever gone
still I walk this lonely road from twelite till dawn
Like a dove up in the blue that has lost his mate
I know I'll never find you but still I search and wate

III

The flowers she planted when love was true have withdrow & died
The house we planed is dark and cold without her love inside
All the joy's of life are gone there's nothing left but pain
as I walk the lonely road of life and search but all in vain —

IV

Sometimes I stop and tell my self there's no use to pretend
no matter how long the road someware there's an end
Then I'll here the whisel blow of a lonesome train
and my journey starts anew searching but in vain —

Jan 17, 1951
Hank Williams

("Mansion for your Soul")

I

If you chose the road of sin my Brother
you will have to pay the toll
you may have a mansion for your body
But do you have a mansion for your soul—

II

oh the good book says to love your brother
help him out when he gets in a hole.
Then when you leave this world true what you
youll find a mansion for your soul—

III

you may have a castel lined with marbel
with walls made out of solid gold—
But if God don't live inside your castel
youll still need a mansion for your soul—

IV

In my fathers house there many mansions
many times you've had the story told
But if you never learn to love your saviour
youll never find a mansion for your soul—

V

When the masters Book of life is opened
and the angels start to call the roll—
If you've lived according to his teaching
youll be given a mansion for your soul—

August 14, 1949. Radio Corral, Jim
and Jane's Country Music Park

A grey haired lady

An old grey haired mother lay dieing
she called for her onely son
she said son don't wait till tomorow to
straighten up with Jesus
for tommorow may not come.

Dear friends Dont wait till tomorow
To pay for deed's you have done
get right Today with youre savour
for tomorow may not come

In this sinful world were living
frome god the people all have ran
an god may make Today the payday
an tomorow may not come

In this selfish quest for power
The world forgot the holey one
The have no love for their neighbor
an tomorow may not come

this Wicked world

god so loved the wicked people the wicked mortals
that he gave his only son
but some thing coming or payday
But this world will pay it in full
and tomorow may not come.

People care not for their savour
fathers kill their only son's
daughters stand and curse their mothers
friends tomarrow may not come.

how can this world keep on standing
after all the things its pepoples done
meet god today and not tomarow
for tomarow may not come.

god so loved this Wicked world
that he gave his only son
but this world's fograton he gxt

Most country singers tried to write at least some of their own songs, but none were as prolific or as consistently successful as Hank. Under Fred Rose's tutelage, he became the most accomplished songwriter in Nashville. After Tony Bennett recorded "Cold, Cold Heart" in 1951, most of Hank's singles were also covered by pop singers, doubling Hank's income. He wrote compulsively and continually, his increasingly troubled relationship with Audrey providing much of the inspiration. Success seemed to underscore their differences. She wanted to integrate herself into Nashville society, while he wanted to go fishing.

Hank had never really stopped drinking for long; the months after he arrived in Nashville were probably his longest period of sobriety since his mid-teens. From late 1949 onward, though, Hank resumed binge drinking, which further alienated Audrey—as did the fact that his career, which she had seen as *their* career, now excluded her.

From Hank's notebook: "Tomorrow May Not Come" and "This Wicked World"

Outside Hank and Audrey's Corral

Audrey tried to keep her ambitions alive, recording first for Decca in 1950, then for MGM, but her failure only sharpened the contrast with Hank. "Why Don't You Love Me (Like You Used to Do)," "A House Without Love," and "Why Should We Try Any More?" clearly drew their inspiration from Hank and Audrey's deteriorating marriage.

"It Works One Way or The Other"

If your mama cross and she won't treat right
Beat her every morning and love her every night
Then she'll do right, like a good gal ought to do.
She'll quit her naging, and making you serve

If you family life aint what it ought to be
Then all you gotta do, ~~follow this recipe~~ is take this tip from me
Then ~~you~~ around your house ~~a~~ you'll see a change
Things run smoother, and honey will be your name

If she fusses about every ~~thing you do~~ little thing you do
always getting angry and sassy, and just won't do
show her whose boss, use a strong hand
Then she'll harness that temper, ~~and~~ ~~to~~ do your command

now I tried this out and it worked just fine
I've got no more troubles, ~~since a single man~~ nor worried mind
~~my old gal done left me here behind~~
~~no~~ my old gal has done left me way behind
It works one way are the other every time

"The way I feel is that if you don't like folk music, stay away from my shows. Personally, I cain't stand classical stuff, but I don't tell the world about it. I just turn the radio off. Why cain't these folks who don't like my music do the same? When they start making fun of me, I don't even answer them. I like to think that folk songs express the dreams and prayers and hopes of working people. That's why it makes me mad to hear these popular orchestras make a jazzed up comedy of a religious song like 'Wreck on the Highway.' It ain't a funny song, and Roy Acuff made the first recording of it, and Roy can quote you as much of the Bible as a preacher. I know a few singers who have made over $100,000 a year singing this music. Roy Acuff has been doing it the last fifteen years. They have big homes, but they're still sincere when they sing. These pop bands will only play our hillbilly songs when they cain't eat any other way." (Hank Williams, interviewed in Charleston, South Carolina, March 2, 1951)

"I knew when I was with him that Hank was a great country song-writer, but I never realized he was a great American songwriter. We used to kid him. His billfold was so thick 'cause it was stuffed full of bits and pieces of ideas for songs. We'd say, 'Hoss, be careful, you'll fall off that billfold, break an arm, and we'll have to get us a new lead singer.' He wrote a lot of songs just riding down the highway, beating out a little rhythm on the dashboard. Most times, we didn't have any room to get a guitar out. We'd get a cardboard out from a pressed shirt, and Don Helms or Jerry or me would take the words down. He wrote 'Jambalaya' like that. We were playing down near Monroe, New Iberia—Golden Meadows and Moon Mullican was working with us. We stopped and Don Helms got a sheet of cardboard and Hank and Moon banged that thing back and forth, and Don wrote it down." (Big Bill Lister, June 10, 1992)

"Hank was a poet of the countryside, with a keen insight into human nature and a flashing wit. The people who worked hard for a living loved him. He would dash off a hit tune in a few minutes. He wrote the way he talked. His lines carried terrific wallop of wit and wis-dom. The word 'genius' has been used too much, but if Hank Williams was not a genius, we never saw one." (Opry announcer George D. Hay, broadcast, January 10, 1953)

Where is the love that we once knew
that was so true and divine
where are the words we use to speak
that were so soft and kind
where are the kisses you use to give
so eager and so free
Darling you have grow to Be a Stranger To me

Where is the fun we use to have
just walking hand and hand
where are the thrills we use to get
just dancing to a band
where are the stars that were in your eyes
that I use to see
Darling you have grown to Be a Stranger to me —

Where are the rides we use to take
It seems a million years ago
what has happen to our love
Tell me darling if you know
Where are the moonlight strolls we use to take
down by the rolling sea

PRINCE ALBERT

GRAND OLE OPRY

WSM

SEPTEMBER 22

1951

8:30 - 9:00 P. M.

STARRING: RED FOLEY
              MINNIE PEARL
              ROD BRASFIELD
              THE JORDANAIRES
              STRINGBEAN

SPECIAL GUEST: HANK WILLIAMS

PRINCE ALBERT   PAGE FIVE

JINGLE: THE BITE IS OUT AND THE PLEASURE'S IN
              WHEN YOU SMOKE PRINCE ALBERT
          IT'S SPECIALLY TREATED NOT TO BITE YOUR TONGUE
              THE BITE'S OUT AND THE PLEASURE'S IN!

ANNCR: AND NOW THERE'S MORE TOBACCO IN EVERY POCKET TIN.

FOLEY: I'VE KNOWN SOME FISHERMEN IN MY LIFE, AND I'VE KNOWN SOME SINGERS,
          TOO..BUT I'VE NEVER KNOWN A MAN QUITE LIKE TONIGHT'S PRINCE
          ALBERT GUEST, WHO CAN'T MAKE UP HIS MIND WHETHER HE'D RATHER
          FISH THAN SING, OR SING THAN FISH. BUT I CAN GUARANTEE YOU HE
          DOES BOTH ABOUT AS WELL AS THEY CAN BE DONE. I MEAN THAT GOOD OLE
          LOVE-SICK BLUES BOY, HANK WILLIAMS! ... (APPLAUSE) .. HANK,
          COME UP HERE AND TELL US ALL ABOUT YOURSELF. HEY, AIN'T THAT A
          NEW GUITAR YOU'VE GOT THERE?

HANK: SURE IS RED..

FOLEY: WHAT HAPPENED TO YOUR OLD GUITAR?

HANK: SHUCKS MAN, I NEEDED SOMETHIN' TO KEEP MY BAIT IN!

FOLEY: UMM..I SHOULDN'T'VE ASKED. HANK, SING US THAT SONG O' YOURS
          CALLED "_____". HANK WILLIAMS, FOLKS!

MUSIC: "Hey Good Looking"..HANK WILLIAMS

          APPLAUSE

FOLEY: MAN, THAT SINGIN'S AS PLEASIN' AS A PULL ON A PIPEFUL OF PRINCE
          ALBERT SMOKIN' TOBACCO--RICH, SMOOTH AND FULL-FLAVORED!

          TUNE UP SQUARE DANCE FIDDLE...

                    (FOLEY OVER)

The Grand Ole Opry was broadcast on WSM for its full four hours. But thirty minutes, sponsored by Prince Albert Chewing Tobacco, were networked on NBC and scripted. Here's Hank's dialog with Prince Albert host Red Foley.

The Heavens are lonely Too

The nite is cold and dreary
darling just like your love
vows you made were lies dear
and im blue as the heavens above

I can here the rain a falling
its sounds so lonesome and blue
everything around me looks so dreary
it seems the heavens are lonely To

Black clouds have covered up the moon
The stars refuse to shine
theirs no sunshine left in my life
since you left me here behind

Feb 19, 1947

Oh mama come Home

I wake up this morning
I looked all around
it was then I realized
That you had left this town
Oh mama come, oh mama home
oh mama come home
oh mama come home your daddy is all alone

Theirs no one here now
to warm my bed at nite
All my days are long and sad
and filled with trouble & strife
oh mama come home, oh mama come home,
oh mama come home your daddy is all alone

You're Been Lonesome To —

I

If your heart has known such pain until for death it's cried
Only to have the Lord refuse Then you've been near my side
If in your heart somehow you're no you'll feel what we you do
Then you have walked a road of pain yes you're Been Lonesome to.

II

If you have had each joy of Life destroyed and cast away
Then Watch aloud that once new love grow saddin day by day
If your soul's whithed like a rose, That never felt a dew —
your traveling on the street of grief yes you've been lonesome to

III

If for you wasted wicked life, your soul lives out in shame
and you could live it over again It would never be the same
If you've lived God Please bless the one To whom d was untrue
you've lived a life of regret, yes you're Been Lonesome to.

IV

If when the stars lite up the skies it seems you can't go on
Then out go vision your darling appear you speak but the image is gone
If then the tears came your cheeks There can be no other for you
you can't even hide from Fate. yes you're been lonesome to.

Hank Williams
Nov 22, 1950

"He'd sing these sad songs. 'I just wrote this yesterday,' [he'd say,] and he'd sing it before it was even on record. And the lyrics that would come out of his mouth. Good Lord. He wasn't all that well educated. Where did all this come from? It would scare you." *(Little Jimmy Dickens interviewed by Eddie Stubbs for* Country Boy, *Bear Family Records, 1995)*

"Here's how he came about writing 'Cold, Cold Heart.' I was in the hospital just over some little minor something. We'd had an argument, and he'd come in and I wouldn't even talk to him. We had been in New York, two or three weeks before I went into the hospital, and he'd bought me this fur coat, first fur coat I'd ever owned. Anyway, he said to the housekeeper he was gonna take this fur coat out there to the hospital. I'd talk to the kids, but I wouldn't talk to him. He came back that night and on the way back he said to Hank Jr.'s nurse, 'She's got the coldest heart I ever seen.' Then he came in the den and wrote that song. He got so jealous of men. God knows why. I wasn't doing anything except staying in the background and trying to help him if I could. There was so many stories told. The bigger he got, he always had such a fear of losing me, and I don't know why. I certainly never gave him any reason." *(Audrey Williams interviewed by Dorothy Horstman, 1973)*

Hank maintained that Audrey gave him plenty of reasons to be jealous, and in the cross-complaint filed at the time of their divorce, he stated that Audrey was not in the hospital for "some little minor something" but for a botched abortion.

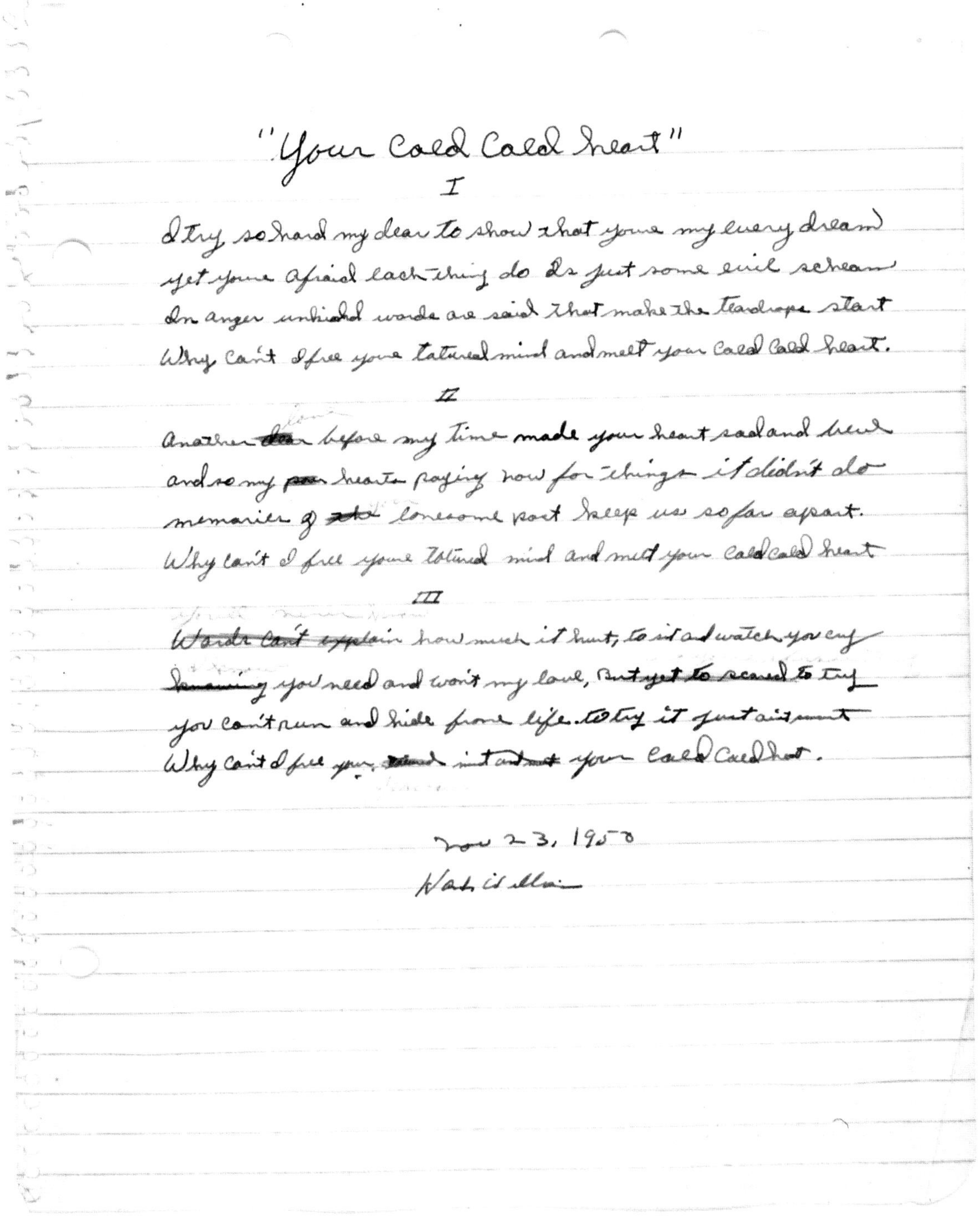

"Your Cold Cold heart"

I

I try so hard my dear to show that your my every dream
yet your afraid each thing do Is just some evil scheam
In anger unkind words are said that make the teardrops start
Why can't I free your tatured mind and melt your cold cold heart.

II

Another dear before my time made your heart sad and blue
and so my poor heart paying now for things it didn't do
memaries of the lonesome past keep us so far apart.
Why can't I free your totued mind and melt your cold cold heart

III

Words can't explain how much it hurt, to sit and watch you cry
knowing you need and want my love, But yet to scared to try
you can't run and hide from life. to try it just ain't want
Why can't I free your stand mit and met your cold cold heart.

Nov 23, 1950
Nashville

With circus giant Ted Evans

With Cesar Romero

THE HADACOL CARAVAN: AUGUST–SEPTEMBER 1951

Between August 14 and October 2, 1951, Hank was scheduled to perform on the Hadacol Caravan, the last great medicine show. Hadacol was the invention of Louisiana state senator Dudley J. LeBlanc. A vaguely fishy tasting mix of vitamins and minerals, its chief ingredient was 12 percent alcohol ("as a preservative").

Hank's first contact with LeBlanc had come in 1949 when he recorded eight radio programs, "the Health and Happiness shows," for LeBlanc's Hadacol corporation. He was just one of many top-ranked stars hired for the 1951 Hadacol Caravan, but he topped the bill nearly every night.

"I have been suffering from nervousness, weak spells, lack of energy, and never felt like working. After taking Hadacol, I am doing my work better than I have in years. I don't have weak spells; I eat well; and I sleep like a log. My little girl didn't eat very much. After taking Hadacol, she eats two helpings every meal. We just can't praise it enough. I just wish more people knew how wonderful Hadacol is." *(Mrs. L. E. Mitchell, Wadsworth, Texas, March 1949)*

"I asked Dudley LeBlanc what was in Hadacol, and he told me there was enough alcohol to make people feel good and enough laxative for a good movement." *(Mercury Records A&R man Murray Nash, 1992)*

"In addition to his own demonstrable vigor, Senator LeBlanc exhibits written testimonials from flourishing invalids in every walk of Dixie life, to prove that by imbibing regularly, their frightening assortment of infirmities, from apoplexy to anemia, have gone down before the restorative onslaught of Hadacol. Whenever medical skeptics call upon him to be more specific, the Senator calls upon LeBlancian logic and gets right to Hadacol's remedial secret: 'It does anything because it's got razor action. If you're fat, it makes you thin. If you're thin, old Haddycol puts meat on ya.'

The Hadacol Goodwill Caravan is the zaniest promotion stunt the seldom unzany patent medicine industry has ever seen. One hundred white and blue Hadacol trucks toured the South's biggest cities. They bring with them the big chief medicine man, his gubernatorial aspirations, and his costly tribe of mercenaries. Every night the Caravan gives an outdoor performance in a different city. Every night, nearly every seat is filled. Every night, the ticket of admission is the same: one Hadacol box top. 'Every place I go,' the Senator said, 'they're drinking Hadacol highballs and jigging to the

(top) Minnie Pearl (left) next to Dudley J. LeBlanc. Hatless Hank is third from right.

(bottom) Although he loved old-time blues music as much as old-time country music, Hank rarely performed with black artists because they didn't appeal to the same crowds, couldn't play the same venues, couldn't eat at the same restaurants, and couldn't stay at the same hotels. The Hadacol Caravan, though, included Sharkey Bonano's Dixieland Band, which featured a black vaudeville dance act, Pork Chops and Kidney Stew. Here, one of them appears to be cartooning old Southern stereotypes or possibly minstrel acts like "Stepin Fetchit."

"Hadacol Boogie." Some places, my audience is twice the town's population. I spent a cool half million for talent, but I sold more than three million bucks worth of Hadacol along the way.'" *(Joseph Roddy, "The Million Dollar Medicine Man," Look magazine, December 5, 1950)*

"A typical Hadacol Caravan show performed at Lakewood Park in Atlanta. The preliminaries started at about 7:30, beginning with the antics of about a dozen acrobatic clowns, doing sleight-of-hand tricks, stunts, and flirtations. The scene included six huge trailer trucks circled in covered wagon fashion and five smaller trucks, one containing a calliope, inside the circle of larger trailers. The main part of the show began with Tony Martin's band playing a Gershwin medley. In this particular show, Cesar Romero acted as master of ceremonies, though Mickey Rooney often did the honors. The acts were as follows: a dance act by the Chez Paree chorus line; several musical selections by Sharkey Bonano and his Dixieland Band; a song-and-dance routine with two New Orleans comic characters, Pork Chops and Kidney Stew; an acrobatic act with Los Gatos; Larry Logan and his harmonica; a comedy routine with Emile Parra; a midget and a circus giant introduced as Mister Before and Mister After; Dick Haymes with several romantic songs; a lady tumbler; Carmen Miranda; the Chez Paree girls again; presentation of the Hadacol beauty contest winners from throughout the South, and awards for the winners of contests with most [Hadacol] box tops. Candy Candido then performed some slapstick comedy; Jack Dempsey appeared in a straight pitchman role to sell Defense Bonds, but with some time devoted to the proposition that LeBlanc would make a great governor of Louisiana. The finale came with a performance by Hank Williams, assisted by country comedian Minnie Pearl." *(From the account of James Harvey Young, published in Floyd Martin Clay's* Coozan Dudley LeBlanc: From Huey Long to Hadacol, *Pelican Publishing, Gretna, Louisiana, 1973)*

"Hank and Minnie were the only country acts. Bob Hope was on the show in Cincinnati, and Hank had been closing the show, but the senator said that because Bob Hope was so expensive he wanted him to close the show. Now Hank encored five times and that crowd wasn't gonna turn him loose, and they were trying to introduce Bob Hope over all this hollerin' and clappin'. They got the crowd quieted down, and somewhere in his wardrobe Bob Hope had this old hat that he'd used in *Paleface,* I guess, and he wore that out and just stood there, and when the place quieted down he said, 'Just call me Hank Hope.' Bob Hope was only with us two shows, and the second night Hank closed the show." (*Big Bill Lister, June 10, 1992*)

(top, left and right) The Caravan in Charlotte, North Carolina, August 28, 1951

(above) Hank and Jack Dempsey fight over Minnie Pearl.

"Those Hadacol shows was when we realized just how big a star Hank was. We thought we were just smalltime, working the sticks, then we saw Hank topping the bill over acts like Bob Hope and Dick Haymes, and we saw just how big he was." *(Don Helms, 1992)*

"I went to see him when the show came to Montgomery. He was on the train, and I sat down beside him. I said, 'Hank, how you doin' boy?' He said, 'I'm doing no good at all.' I said, 'What's the matter? All them pretty movie stars on this train, Hank.' He said, 'I don't have nothin' to do with 'em. They think they're better than I am.' Then he pulled out a pink check about six inches long and three inches high, and it was for something like seventy-five hundred dollars. He said, 'Ever'body on this train has got one of these.' The checks had bounced." *(Braxton Schuffert, December 16, 1992)*

"During the show in Dallas, rumors began to spread that the show was being canceled. Some said [LeBlanc] had run out of money, others that he had sold Hadacol, which proved to be at least near the truth. We planned to have the tour returned to the originating point, Lafayette, Louisiana, but at the very end of the Dallas show the announcement was made that the caravan was officially ended. Everyone was instructed to report to the office car at the train to pick up his transportation ticket home. It was a scene of near panic. Everyone was rushing about trying to get his personal belongings, and at the same time looking for friends made on the tour for one last goodbye." *(Jerry Rivers in* From Life to Legend, *Heather Publications, Denver, CO, 1967)*

LeBlanc had used the Caravan as a smokescreen to hide the true picture of Hadacol's finances and sold the corporation to the Tobey Maltz Company for just $250,000 while the tour was in progress. In 1952, Hadacol was officially declared bankrupt.

(top, left) On stage in Columbus, Ohio, September 5, 1951

(top, right) With two Hadacol dancers in Macon, Georgia, August 24, 1951

MASTER NUMBER 50-S-6009 - 90 R
CATALOG NUMBER 10630 B
RELEASE DATE Release # 76 - 3/24/50
DATE RECORDED January 10th, 1950
ALBUM TITLE
NUMBER
PLACE AND STUDIO NUMBER: Castle Recording Nashville, Tenn.
RECORDING ENGINEER:
TITLE: THE FUNERAL
PLAYING TIME: 3:03
SOURCE: Fred Rose
STUDIO TIME: 2 PM to 5 PM
COMPOSER:
DIRECT RECORDING: XX **FILM TO DISC:**
AUTHOR:
PUBLISHER: Music: MILENE MUSIC
Poem is Public Domain
LICENSE OBTAINED: Fred Rose
COPYRIGHT DATE: **SESAC:** **OTHER:**
ASCAP: XX **BMI:** **A. & R. REP.:** Fred Rose
ARTIST: LUKE THE DRIFTER
CONDUCTOR: With Musical Accompaniment
ACCOMPANIMENT: Poem read by Luke The Drifter
DESCRIPTION:
INSTRUMENTAL SOLOISTS:
REMARKS: Background music: "A House Built On A Rock"

In addition to his regular recordings released under his own name, Hank recorded a series of narrations released as "Luke the Drifter." Narrations were a tradition—albeit fading—embedded deep in country music. There was no serious attempt to hide the fact that "Luke the Drifter" was Hank Williams. The narrations were only issued under a pseudonym to prevent jukebox operators from ordering them; they were, Hank said, "designed for the take-home trade." It might have been a dying tradition, but Hank took pride in his ability to deliver a good narration, adapting some of them from old poems. In releasing them without much fanfare, MGM was indulging Hank, because sales were generally very poor.

"Hank had a deep personal feeling for his fellow man. This didn't show on the outside. You had to get to know him, and then he'd give himself away every now and again about his deep concern for people who were less fortunate. 'The Funeral' touched him. When he did it, he lost himself in it. Him and Don [Helms] finished it with tears rollin' down their faces." *(Guitarist Bob McNett, 1995)*

Career and marital stress, together with increasingly severe back pain, were leading Hank to resume drinking. Sometimes he could wrestle down his addiction; sometimes not. Almost as soon as he started, he would become unable to work and would be brought home from touring.

"[Promoter] A. V. Bamford had Hank Williams and I together for two weeks [in early April 1951]. We flipped coins to see who would go on first. Dad was still driving for us, and there's enough stories to fill a book there. All Hank thought about was writing. He recorded a number he wrote because I was having trouble with my better half called 'I'm Sorry for You, My Friend.' We'd swap songs we'd written. He was the bluest and lonesomest man I ever met. When he and I were down in Corpus Christi, I brought in a bottle of bourbon and set it down in there. We were sitting back getting ready for the show, and I said, 'Hey, I'm gonna have a shot; how about it, do you want a little shot?' He said, 'No, if I had just what you are fixing to take, if I had that, I'd want another and the first thing you know I'd be gone.' I thought he was kidding, but I found out later he really would have. I worked two weeks with him, and he never sung better. He was in good shape, but that was just it, he didn't take a drink, and he put on a SHOW. He was an entertainer. He would take control. He had that ability." (*Lefty Frizzell on* Hank Williams...Reflections by Those Who Loved Him, *MGM Records, 1975*)

"I brought him home from Canada one time [because he was drunk]. I took the little car and left the stretch limo for the boys. I had quite a bit of money in the briefcase. We stopped one morning just after daylight, and I said, 'Hank, you gotta have something to eat, son.' He said, 'Big 'un, I just can't do it.' I knew better than to let him wait in the car, so I just jumped up and paid the bill, and by the time I was out there, he was nowhere to be seen. In the middle of the next block a big sign said 'Cocktails,' and I just broke into a dead run, and by the time I got there, he'd already had him one. I paid his bill and drug him back to the car. It just broke your heart, but I knew I had to get him home. When I got to the edge of town, I called Miss Audrey. I said, 'I'm at the edge of town, and I got Hank with me and he's in pretty bad shape. I just wanted you to be expecting us.' It was maybe five in the morning, and I didn't just want to drive up there to the house. She said, 'I don't care what you do with the son-of-a-bitch, just don't bring him out here.' So I called [Opry manager] Jim Denny, and Jim told me where to take him—the hospital out in Madison. Then I went by the studio and put the money in the safe, then around nine o'clock Audrey called me and wanted to know where her money was at. I said, 'Lady, as far as I know you ain't got no damn money. I gave Hank's money to Jim.' The man was in bad shape, and he needed tender love and care, but he couldn't get it—he just got the hut." (*Big Bill Lister, June 10, 1992*)

"They had a sanitarium in Madison with some out-buildings and bars on the windows. Hank called it 'the hut.' We'd pull up and someone would say, 'Come on, Hank, let's get out,' and he'd see where we were and say, 'Oh no, oh no, I ain't goin' in there. It's that damn hut.' Then the attendants would have to come and get him, and he'd stare daggers at us. Seems to me that everyone would disappear round about that time, but I lived close-by and I'd known Hank the longest. I'd come visit after a couple of days, bring candy bars and books. By the third day, Hank would say, 'Reckon they're gonna let us outta here?' I'd think, 'Hoss, *we* ain't in here." (*Don Helms, 1992*)

The Drunkards Dream

I

I dreamed that my dear mother so sweet
With her last breath was praying for me
Dear god please save my precious boy
fill his heart with heavens joy

II

Dear god please show him right from wrong
I cant help him now for I must go home
O lord we failed but you know I tried
With a tear on her cheek my mother died

III

My daddy was their holding to her hand
When death angel took her to that great land
he looked so alone and hepless their
With mothers last words ringing in his ear

IV

I hard awake from my drunken dream
The world had turned dark it seemd
And then In my wicked heart I knew
That all of my drunken dream was true.

V

I hurried to my mothers side
With Burning Tears in my eyes
my dad was weeping by her bed
Because my mother dear was dead

VI

Dear God up their in heaven
Please here this sinful drunkards prayer
Ill mother dear I see the way
And that Ill meet her some glad day

Nov 24 1947

By the end of 1951, the pressure of constant touring and the necessity of keeping the hit streak alive were taking their toll on Hank. In October he was in New York for an appearance on the Perry Como show, staying in a hotel on Times Square. Possibly watched by minders assigned to keep him from drinking, as was often the case at that time, he had little to do but write another song.

King Edward Hotel

44TH STREET EAST OF BROADWAY

NEW YORK

CABLE ADDRESS "KINGEDOTEL"

I Thank My God for you

I

When this cruel world has been unkind
And left me sad and blue
Its then I kneeld in umble prayer
and I Thank my god for you -

You allways met with open arms
to under stant each thing I do
and lend your hand when I am down
and I thank my god for you

III

The understanding in your eyes
and love so kind and true
Makes me the ritches man on earth
and I thank my god for you

I pray to god to give me strenght
so praises wont be to few
for your my dreams my love my life
and I thank my god for you.

Hank Williams

Oct 11, 1951, Kn hotel, N.y. york
city

In December 1951, Hank disbanded the Drifting Cowboys and went into Vanderbilt Medical Center for an operation on his spine. He was scheduled to make some New Year's appearances in the D.C. area but sent Audrey in his place.

"We knew he couldn't make the show, so [the Opry] and Jim Denny started talking about me going in his place—and I did. He wouldn't have been able to get out of bed that early, and we were afraid people might think he was intoxicated. He started acting up before I left, and I took the children and left. There were three elderly women came back home with me, so I could get some clothes and fly to Washington. I just wanted to slip in and out. We were just easin' around, and I knew he was there and very edgy, and as we were leaving the gun shot four times. I could hardly walk, I was scared to death. Thinking back, I don't know if he was shooting at me or wanting me to think that he was shooting at himself. Anyway, I went on to Washington, and New Year's Eve night I called him and said, 'Hank, I'll never live with you another day.'" (Audrey Williams, undated interview)

"What Can a heart do"

I

What can a heart say
I hats broken and blue
No one to cry to
so what can it do—
no one to love now
no use to try
what can a heart do
just pray to die—

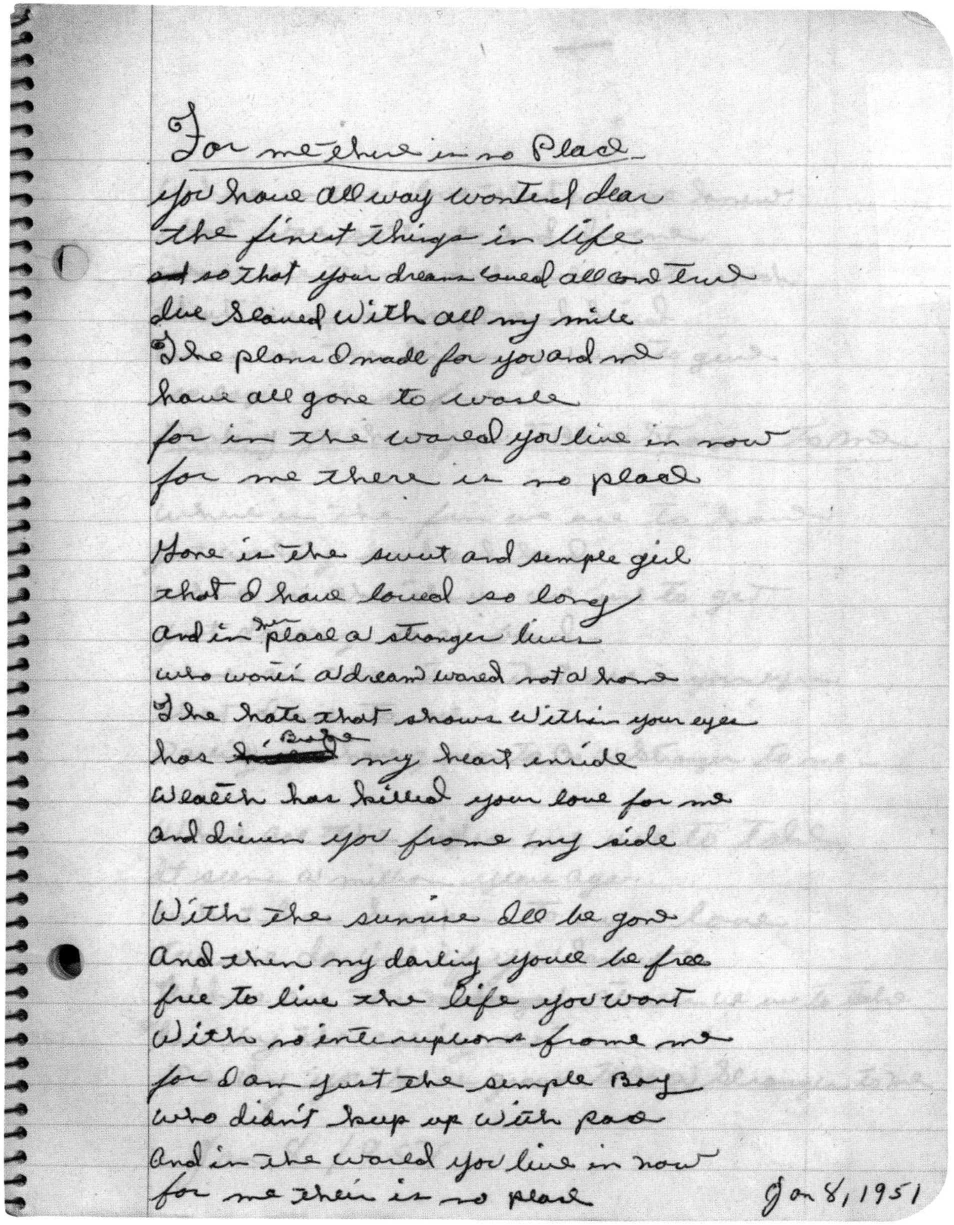

For me there is no Place

you have all way wanted dear
the finest things in life
and so that your dream could all come true
I've slaved with all my mite
The plans I made for you and me
have all gone to waste
for in the world you live in now
for me there is no place

Gone is the sweet and simple girl
that I have loved so long
And in her place a stranger lives
who would a dreamd wanted not a home
The hate that shows within your eyes
has broke my heart inside
Wealth has killed your love for me
and driven you from my side

With the sunrise I'll be gone
And then my darling you'll be free
free to live the life you want
With no interruptions from me
for I am just the simple Boy
who didn't keep up with pace
And in the world you live in now
for me there is no place

Jan 8, 1951

(I'm so Tired of it All)
All my life I've been so lonesome
if happiness came I missed the call
All my dreams have died and vanished
And now I'm so tierd of it All

In life and love I've been a failure
to many tears thrue it all
to many broken vows and promises
and now I'm so tierd of it all

Every thing I ever loved I lost it
to many times I've watched my castles fall
my life is full of regreting
And now I'm so tierd of it all

frome this world I'll soon be goneing
no one will miss me after all
up their I pray I'll find contenment
for now I'm so tierd of it all

June 29, 1947

6 "I'M SO TIRED OF IT ALL": JANUARY—JUNE 1952

The year 1952 would be the last of Hank Williams' brief life. Now wracked by almost ceaseless back pain, which the operation in December 1951 had done little to alleviate, he curtailed personal appearances and slowly lost interest in his career. His marriage was ending, and he often seemed to lack the competitiveness that had once driven him. Sometimes, though, he was rivetingly on form, still the most compelling and charismatic act in country music, and he was charting as many hits as ever. He never again had a regular band, picking up musicians whenever he had a showdate. In January, after leaving the family home on Franklin Road, he moved briefly to a hotel while Audrey filed for divorce.

"A year to the night before he died, I told him I would never live with him again. Six months to the day when we got our divorce, he told me, 'Well, I've done everything I can do. I've paid men off to say they've been to bed with you. I've done everything to get you back.' You know what the problem was? I had these two children. I said, 'These children have to have a mother.' I could see they wasn't gonna have a father. He got so far gone, God bless his heart, that they just got nervous when he walked in the door. And that's bad on children. Everybody always said, 'He's gonna kill you one of these days.' He'd do these things and when he'd come to his senses, he'd put his head on my lap and cry just like a baby. He'd say, 'Why do I do that to you? I know better 'n that. Why do I do it? Why do I do it?' I begged him to go to a psychiatrist. I said, 'We'll just close the house up, and we'll rent an apartment, and we'll stay close to you.' He told me, 'If you ever have me put anywhere, I'll kill you.' He needed help so bad, and I just couldn't do it."

(Audrey Williams interviewed by Dorothy Horstman, 1973)

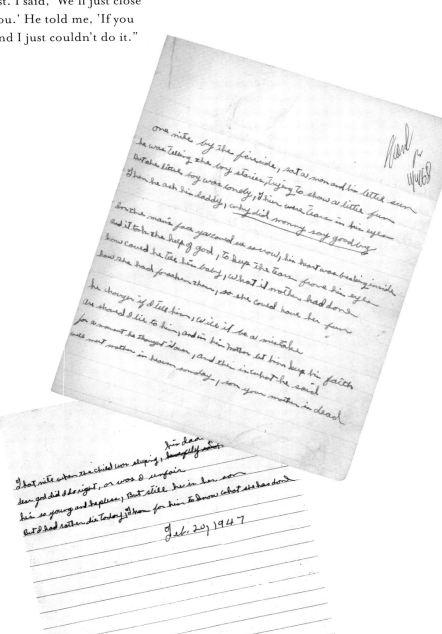

"[I] have suffered every humiliation, abuse and mistreatment that a man could possibly take from a woman....[She] refused to appreciate the obligations of married life, denying her attentions and affections, insisting that she too was a singer and entertainer of ability. [She] has always been possessed of an ungovernable temper, and would fly into fits and rages....[She] has never kept her home as a wife and mother should, she has never stayed at home, notwithstanding the fact that she was furnished with every convenience and every luxury money could buy. She has always insisted on traveling about, acting independent, free of all marital restraint and obligation, seeking and having everything she wanted, and a good time all the time....Against [my] better judgment, I have spent thousands of dollars hoping [I] could capture her interest and keep her at home, which she would preside over as a wife and mother. In return, she continuously refers to [me] as a 'son-of-a-bitch' and many other names too vile and vulgar to mention....She has cursed and abused [me], thrown furniture, and inflicted violence upon [me] in almost every conceivable fashion....In January 1952, [she] was apprehended by police officers in an automobile on a side road in Davidson County, Tennessee, behind the municipal airport. The car was parked with lights out and under cover of darkness at a secluded spot. She was in the company of an automobile dealer, and she was in his arms, and he was loving and kissing her." (*Answer and Cross Bill of the Defendant, Hank Williams, in* Audrey Williams vs. Hank Williams, *1952*)

(Honkey Tonkin mama)
Listen to me little gal
you better quit your fooling around
youre daddys getting tired
of the way youre running round
honkey tonkin honkey tonkin mama

I took you out of a honkey tonk
and gave you a home
but every time I turn my back
you are out an gone
honkey tonkin honkey tonkin mama

you look so innocent
when I look into your eyes
but ever time you open your mouth
I know youre gona lie
honkey tonkin honkey tonkin mama

your baby face and big blue eyes
made me believe in you
but hang around a honkey tonk
is all you won't to do
honkey tonkin honkey tonkin mama

you slep allday and prowl allnight
youre just like a owl
out scrooching with another guy
youre a two timming gal
honkey tonkin honkey tonkin mama

you said you loved me
by all the stars above
but baby honkey tonkin
done got in your blood
honkey tonkin honkey tonkin mama

June 29, 1947

Hank tried to perform in January 1952, but the results were disastrous.

"After a half-hour, Ray Price announced that 'Hank had a serious operation on his spine about nine weeks ago, but he made this engagement, so here he is.' Hank came in, his spine most certainly not holding him erect. He sang 'Cold, Cold Heart,' but did not get some of the words in the right places. Then he sang 'Lovesick Blues' with a good deal of off-key yodeling. Several couples got up and left the auditorium. Then Hank sang 'Lonesome Whistle.' Some more people got up. Hank walked off and intermission was called. It lasted twenty-five minutes. Ray Price and his boys came back. Half the audience applauded their stalwart efforts to keep the show going. The other half yelled for Hank to come back. Presently, Price was called offstage. When he came back, he said, 'The situation seems a lot improved,' and introduced Hank to the crowd again. The audience greeted him with laughs and a few boos, to which he answered, 'I wish I was in as good shape as you are. Hank Williams is a lot of things, but he ain't a liar. If they's a doctor in the house, I'll show him I've been in the hospital for eight weeks and this is my first show since then. And if you ain't nice to me I'll turn around and walk off.' Price, who deserved some special place in Hillbilly Heaven, said, 'We all love you, Hank, don't we folks?' and the audience applauded and laughed. Then Hank sang 'Move It on Over' and it sounded almost as good as one of his records after it has been played a few hundred times. As a finish, he sang 'Cold, Cold Heart,' remembering all the words. Then he walked out and got in his big yellow automobile." *(Elizabeth Lindemann in the Richmond, Virginia,* Times Dispatch, *January 30, 1952)*

Canceling all showdates, Hank returned to Montgomery.

"During the spring of '52, Hiram called me and asked me to come to his mother's house in Montgomery and bring him back to my home in McWilliams. I was surprised when I parked near the house because they were carrying Hiram on a stretcher and putting him in the ambulance from St. Jude's Hospital. I followed them to the hospital and to Hiram's room, but wasn't able to talk to him because he was unconscious. I told the doctor the boy had called me earlier that day and asked me to come get him. The doctor told me to leave Hiram at the hospital until he could get the dope out of him. He said he had enough dope in him to kill a mule. Then the boy's mother said that he had only two beers and two aspirins all day. The doctor asked if she was sure it was aspirin." *(Lon Williams interviewed by Harry E. Rockwell, August 1969)*

Hank returned to Nashville in February or March, renting a house that he shared with newcomer Ray Price. He slowly began broadcasting and scheduling personal appearances, but to ease the discomfort of long journeys, he chartered an aircraft flown by Minnie Pearl's husband, Henry Cannon.

(above, left) Hank with Sammy Pruett (seated) and Grady Martin

(above, right) Hank and Sammy Pruett

(far left) On March 11, 1952, Hank was broadcasting from WSM Studio C. Two fans from Kansas, Floyd Williams (left) and his cousin, Francis Williams, snapped the only known photos of Hank in the studio.

(left) Don Helms

On March 26 and again on April 23, 1952, Hank appeared coast-to-coast on *The Kate Smith Evening Hour,* a television variety show. He was devastatingly on-form for both appearances: confident, assured, and healthy. The kinescopes (film shot from a studio monitor) survived; they remain the only high quality Hank Williams performance footage. During rehearsals, Hank wrote another song, "You'll Never Again Be Mine."

In April 1952, between the Kate Smith shows, Hank was in California. In the past, he had rarely ventured out West, usually staying within driving distance of the Opry, but a large audience of Southerners had relocated out there, and now that he was not employing a regular band, he could fly out by himself, pick up a band, and play for his fans. The California trip ended with Hank falling off the wagon.

"I took a flight out to San Diego. It was going to be Tubb and Williams. We were playing the auditorium there. The boys were worried that Hank was ill and unable to perform. They kinda insisted that he perform, and it made me kinda unhappy. Then I walked backstage, and they were bringing him up the steps, and the look he had on his face was of such implication that I never will forget it. He said, 'Minnie, I can't work. I can't work, Minnie. Tell 'em.' I had no authority. They went ahead, and he worked and it was bad. Promoter A.V. Bamford told me to stay with him between shows. He said, 'He may listen to you. You may be able to keep him from getting any worse than he is.' Maxine Bamford and Hank and me and someone else drove around with him. This was between shows, and we were trying to keep him from getting anything else that would make him get in worse shape than he was. We started singing. He was all hunkered down, looking out of the side of the car singing. He was singing, 'I Saw the Light,' then he stopped and he turned around, and his face broke up and he said, 'Minnie, I don't see no light. There ain't no light.'" *(Minnie Pearl on* Hank Williams...Reflections by Those Who Loved Him, *MGM Records, 1975)*

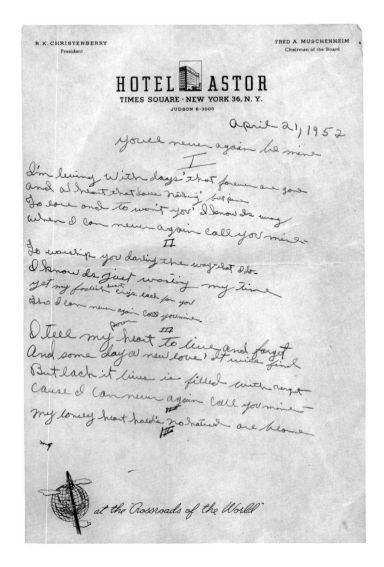

Vallée-Video

6611 SANTA MONICA BLVD., HOLLYWOOD 38, CALIFORNIA

April 25, 1952

Mr. Hank Williams
c/o WSM
Natl. Life & Accident Ins. Co.
301 7th Avenue N.
Nashville, Tennessee

My dear Hank:

First I would like to thank you very sincerely for getting me my MGM deal.

Sorry I didn't see you at the Knickerbocker. We called, but you had left, and my throat was giving me a bad time since the operation, and on learning of your back trouble, I can only wish you good riddance of your ailment.

Next time you're here, how about letting me know. Skaletar is my pal and doctor. I've had to cancel out a month's bookings, and I'm getting a little worried, but I hope that the voice will return in the next few days. It's been two weeks since the operation.

I'm enclosing a song written by a good Yale friend of mine who makes wonderful photo copies. In fact I am asking him to make a batch of little wallet-size photos for you (per the one enclosed) if you will send him one of your best glossies. He does all my work, and has the best price.

Again, Hank, my thanks, and best to your boys.

Sincerely,

RUDY VALLÉE

While in California, Hank renewed his acquaintance with crooner Rudy Vallee, who had worked with him on the Hadacol Caravan. Vallee's 1932 recording of "Brother, Can You Spare a Dime?" virtually defined the Depression era, but thirty years later he wasn't doing so well. Stylistically, he and Hank had little in common, but they appear to have enjoyed each other's company.

(above) With San Jose songwriter Johnny Pusateri

(left) Hank with a fan in San Jose, California, April 1952

Hank had re-signed with MGM Records in September 1951, and the contract was broadened to motion pictures. On June 16, 1952, Hank was back in California for a screen test. He met MGM Pictures' head of production, Dore Schary, but the meeting did not go well. The following day, the motion picture contract was terminated.

"Hank had initially been interested in making a good impression on Schary, but alcohol always tended to bring out an antisocial streak in him. Inside the office, he did a 180-degree somersault. He didn't bother to take his hat off, although it might have been because he didn't want the producer to know how bald he was. But then as Schary, who was rather pompous and condescending, began to talk, Hank leaned back his chair, pulled his hat over his eyes and stuck his boots up on Schary's desk. When he attempted to question Hank and got only grunts, he quickly got the message." (*Wesley Rose quoted in Arnold Rogers and Bruce Gidoll,* The Life and Times of Hank Williams, *Haney-Jones Books, Nashville, TN, 1993*)

METRO-GOLDWYN-MAYER PICTURES

C U L V E R ~ C I T Y
CALIFORNIA

June 17, 1952

Mr. Hank Williams,
c/o Mr. Fred Rose,
220 Capitol Building,
Nashville 3, Tenn.

Dear Mr. Williams:

Referring to that certain contract between you and us
dated September 22, 1951 covering your employment by
us as an actor in such roles and in such photoplays
and/or other productions as we may designate, this is
to notify you that, for good and sufficient cause,
your employment under said contract is hereby terminated.

It is intended by this notice to terminate your employment only under the particular contract hereinbefore
referred to dated September 22, 1951 which relates to
your employment as an actor in such roles and in such
photoplays and/or other productions as we may designate
and this notice does not terminate or otherwise affect
your employment under any other contract or agreement
heretofore entered into between you and us.

Yours very truly,

LOEW'S INCORPORATED

BY_____
                Vice President

ama:ea

Bobbie Jett (fourth from right)

Bobbie Jett and her mother in Nashville

Back in Nashville, the divorce was proceeding. Hank and Audrey had lived on the brink, but there would be no going back this time. Hank, meanwhile, had a new girlfriend, Bobbie Jett. A year older than Hank, she had been a dancer but was working as a secretary when they met. She already had a young daughter, Josephine, born in 1948, apparently during a brief marriage to Western B-movie star Monte Hale. By June, Bobbie was three months pregnant with Hank's child.

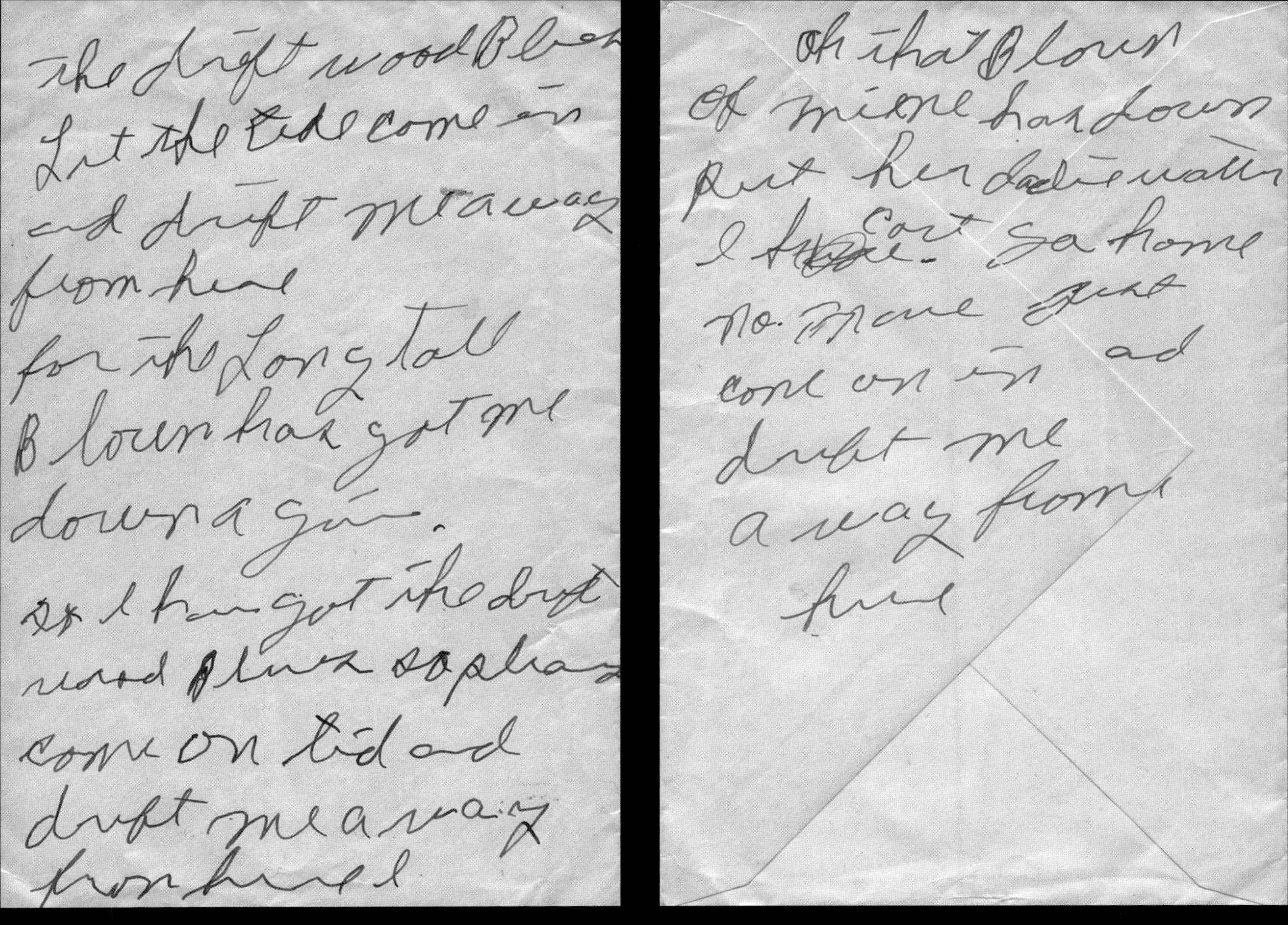

the drift wood Blu
Let the tide come in
and drift me away
from here
for the Long tall
B lover has got me
down a gin.

♪ I have got the drift
wood Blues so bad
come on tid and
drift me away
from here

Oh that I lover
Of mine has gone
Put her suitcase
I can't go home
no more just
come on in and
drift me
a way from
here

A scrawled song fragment, never even submitted
by Hank to his music publisher.

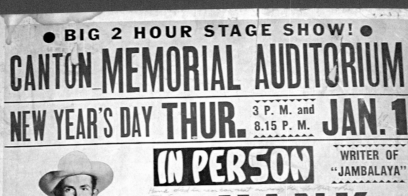

● BIG 2 HOUR STAGE SHOW! ●

CANTON MEMORIAL AUDITORIUM

NEW YEAR'S DAY THUR. 3 P.M. and 8.15 P.M. JAN. 1

IN PERSON

WRITER OF "JAMBALAYA"

HANK WILLIAMS

"MR. LOVESICK BLUES ★ STAR OF M G M RECORDS & FILMS

PLUS THESE GREAT RADIO & T V FAVORITES

IN THE BIGGEST **JAMBOREE** OF 1953

HOMER & JETHRO

RCA - VICTOR RECORDING ARTIST STARS OF THE WLS NATIONAL BARN DANCE & SPIKE JONES' TV SHOWS!

HAWKSHAW HAWKINS

RDS OF PERSONALITY ★ KING RECORDS ★ ABC RADIO JAMBOREE

● AUTRY INMAN from "GRAND OLE OPRY"
● MERLE "RED" TAYLOR ★ JACK and DANIEL
● The Beautiful WEBB SISTERS and MANY OTHERS!

RESERVED SEATS Adults $1.50 - Children 75c ● Tickets A STARK'S
GEN. M. ADULTS $1.25 - CHILDREN 80c

POSTERS INC., 835 Cherry St., Phila.

7 "THEN CAME THAT FATAL DAY": JUNE—DECEMBER 1952

Hank's star continued to rise even as his life unraveled. Often, he seemed to be his old self. He never faltered in the studio, never recorded sub-par material, and, as a result, his records were still selling exceptionally well. On June 13, 1952, he recorded "Jambalaya," which would become his second biggest hit after "Lovesick Blues." The following night he met Billie Jean Jones, who would become his second wife. Strikingly beautiful, she had lived on the same street as he had in Shreveport.

Billie Jean Eshliman Jones

Although a fake poster was widely circulated after Hank's death, this is the poster for the show Hank never gave.

"I've seen cars smash into each other when Billie Jean was walking down the street. No kidding, smash into each other."

(Merle Kilgore, songwriter, Louisiana Hayride star, and—later—Hank Jr.'s manager)

"I was in senior high school when I met my first husband. He was in the Air Police. I met him because he was working with my father, who was a policeman. I was 17. I thought I was in love. My husband-to-be was 19, and we married and I quit school. And we had a child, a girl. Right after my marriage, my husband was transferred to Lubbock, Texas. At that time, he was a corporal. I went with him, pregnant, and our rent was $90 a month. I stayed until I was eight months pregnant. We lived right in the middle of a cotton patch. We picked cotton in his off-duty hours, but I was getting so large that I had to quit and come back home to live with my parents in order to have the baby. Since I had no education to speak of, the only thing I could do was carhop or cocktail waitress, and I was working all night until six in the morning, going home and caring for my baby in the daytime.

"From there, I went to the telephone company as an operator. Then, I realized I wasn't really in love, so I filed for separation. I met a singer from my home town, Shreveport, Louisiana, Faron Young, and started to date him a lot. He got the chance to appear on the Grand Ole Opry as a guest, and I went with him. We made plans to marry, but I couldn't get along with Faron. No one can. I had applied for a transfer from the telephone company in Shreveport to the telephone company in Nashville, and by the time it came through Faron and I were on the outs, but I had to take my transfer.

"The first night I got into Nashville I went to the Grand Ole Opry with Faron, and I was sitting in the guest box when Hank came in. This was the early summer of 1952. He asked me if I was married, and I said, 'No sir.' He said, 'Well, who you with?' I told him I was there with Faron Young. He sent for Faron. He said, 'Boy, are you gonna marry this girl?' Faron said, 'No sir, I don't think so. She's got too many boyfriends for me.' Kidding like. So he says, 'Well, if you don't, I am.' He says, 'Let's all go out to a club after the show.' I said, 'I really don't want to go' because I had been traveling all day and all night from Shreveport, which is like fifteen hours. But Faron was afraid of Hank because Hank was king of the singers. So we went to the club, and I says, 'Well, I won't go in because I don't drink.' So Hank says, 'Well, I'll just sit out in the car with you, and Faron and my girl can go on in and

Hank and Billie pictured during their engagement.

dance.' Hank and I talked about home because he'd lived in Shreveport about four houses from me.

"By this time I had gotten an apartment, a ten-dollar-a-week apartment because that's all I could afford. It was lopsided. You had to walk kinda crooked to walk through it. After that night, he started coming over all the time and he seemed to get a big kick just sitting there drinking coffee in my lopsided apartment.

"[Two months later] we went home to tell my mother that we were going to marry. We hired a chauffeur who drove us to Shreveport to tell my mom and dad. On the way back, we stopped to get some fish, and the chauffeur was going to cook the fish at Hank's house. When we got there, one of his girlfriends had moved in, literally bag and baggage. She broke the door out and she moved in. Here I am with my fiancé, and this blonde had moved in. He asked her to leave and she wouldn't. That was the only kind of people that was around him. I said, 'Well, I'm leaving. Just have the chauffeur take me home.' I said, 'I'm tired of the blondes, I'm tired of the whiskey, I'm tired of the whole bit.' The blonde left before I left. He picked her up and bodily threw her out down the stairs and out the front door. She would get up and come back in. So they all loaded in the car, and, if you can believe it, she went too. They all took me home. He walked me to the door, took me in, and said he would get rid of her and be back. I said, 'Nope, just do me a favor and let me alone. I've enjoyed all of this relationship I can stand.' I was on the Greyhound bus the next morning going home." (*Billie Jean Williams Berlin, deposition, December 13, 1968, re. Civil Action No. 12,181,* Billie Jean Williams Berlin vs. MGM Inc.)

The Greenville Homecoming. Hank is joined by his mother (back seat), his cousin Marie Harvell's son, Lewis Fitzgerald (front seat), and his father (standing beside the car to the right). The driver might be Charles Carr, who drove Hank on his final ride. Hank purchased the Cadillac on the day of the homecoming.

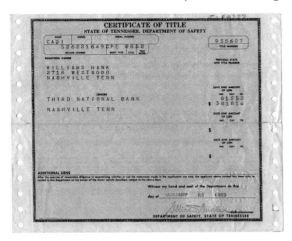

Shortly after Billie Jean left, Hank went into a tailspin, drinking again and skipping Opry dates. The Opry's policy had always been that no artist was bigger than the show, and by missing the Saturday night Opry and Opry-promoted concerts, Hank was damaging its reputation. On August 11, 1952, he was fired.

"I was with Hank when he got fired. [Opry manager] Jim Denny told him he was going to have to let him go. He had a check coming, about three hundred dollars. He said, 'You cain't fire me 'cause I already quit.' Jim asked Hank if anyone was there with him, and Hank said, 'Johnnie Wright's here.' He said, 'Tell Johnnie I want to talk to him.' I got on the phone and Jim said, 'Johnnie, he's got a check up here. You come by and pick it up.' My brother-in-law had a Chrysler limousine and Hank had his trailer with Drifting Cowboys written on the side. We put all his belongings in the trailer and his reclining chair in the back of the limousine and put him in there. We got Hank in the car and went up to WSM. Roy Acuff and Owen Bradley was in Jim Denny's office. Roy said, 'Have you got Hank out there?' I said, 'Yeah.' Owen said, 'Let's go out and see him, Roy.' They went out and I picked up his check. Then we took off to Montgomery. He was coming off a drunk. We drove down Broadway and [passed] a liquor store…and Hank said, 'Johnnie, pull in there and get me some whiskey.' So I pulled in and got him a fifth and cashed his three hundred dollar check. We took him to his mother's house." (*Johnnie Wright of Johnnie and Jack, December 18, 1992*)

"They fired me from the Opry, but when I'm on the road, who closes the show?"
(*Hank to his cousin Walter McNeil, August 1952*)

On August 15, 1952, Hank performed at a second homecoming, this one in Greenville, Alabama. He went to Nashville that morning to collect his pregnant girlfriend, Bobbie Jett.

"Hank introduced me to the pretty blonde that was with him. He introduced her to me as 'Bobbie Blue.' Bobbie went with us to Kowaliga Bay on Lake Martin. I left them there. Around midnight, the telephone rang and the Alexander City Police were on the line. Hank was in jail and could I come down? I was allowed to go back and get him, still asleep. I slung him across my shoulder, took him outside and laid him in the back seat of his Cadillac. We headed down the Dadeville Highway towards a motel. I got a room for Bobbie and Hank. We got Hank to bed. Bobbie asked me if I wouldn't mind taking her down to the lake to get some things. While Bobbie and I were at the lake house, I heard her crying and throwing up. I asked her what was wrong, and she said she was pregnant. I drove Bobbie back to the hotel and headed home again….Wednesday afternoon, we all loaded up and drove back to Lake Martin to Kowaliga. As the night passed, we continued to have a bit of a party. When refreshments ran out, we drove to a bootlegger in Kellyton. All the way up there, Hank was saying, 'Bob, I feel a song building up. I just have the strangest feeling about it. It's such a beautiful place. I keep thinking about the Indians, the water….' As we left the [bootlegger's] house, we hit a bad bump. Hank fell forward and hit the Cadillac's leather dashboard. He started pounding out some rhythm on the dash, 'Kawliga, kawliga.' He looked over at me, saying, 'Hurry, Bob, get back to the lake. I've got it. I know what I want now.'" (*Deejay Bob McKinnon, unpublished reminiscence*)

The Kowaliga fishing lodge where Hank wrote "Kaw-Liga"

Hometown reporter Allen Rankin, who would later help Lillie write a factually fast-and-loose book about Hank, was protective of Hank in this report of his return to Greenville.

"To get out of Nashville, Hank dropped his Grand Ole Opry spot on WSM and disappeared southward leaving an ex-wife, two children, a mansion, and, it is said, fifty percent of his song royalties....His two remaining Cadillacs, a blue convertible and a tan coupe, stood quietly in front of his mother's boarding house at 318 North McDonough. Inside, Hank too lay still for a while....A few weeks ago, the great hillbilly song publisher, Fred Rose, arrived quietly at the Williams' boarding house. 'Mr. Rose and Hank just sat there in that front room and talked and wrote songs and talked and wrote songs until late into the night,' recalls Hank's mother. 'Sometime late in the night, I woke up and heard the prettiest song I ever heard. They'd already put it on tape and recorded it, and they were playing it back. It was so pretty, it made my hair stand up on end.'" (*The* Montgomery Advertiser, *September 28, 1952*)

The song that moved Lillie so profoundly was probably "Your Cheatin' Heart."

Rose pulled some strings to get Hank back on the Louisiana Hayride, and in September, he returned to Shreveport. It had been just three years since he left there in triumph for Nashville. Bobbie Jett remained in one of Lillie's boarding houses, and Hank immediately resumed his relationship with Billie Jean.

"[Back in August] we had set the date of our marriage for October 18TH [but] by then I didn't expect to ever hear from him again. Then he called me and he said, 'We have a date on October 18TH.' And he was sober. He said, 'I'll be down there in a couple of days.' In a few days, here he came with his [new] manager, Clyde Perdue, and both his cars.

"A promoter that's well known for making a quick dollar, Oscar Davis, came down and he knew that Hank and I were getting married. He said, 'Why don't we make some money out of this thing? Why don't we have a public wedding?' Oscar Davis could make probably twenty thousand dollars [on the wedding]. So Hank said, 'What do you say?' I said, 'Well, it doesn't matter to me where we get married, really.' Oscar handled all the details. Big formal wedding in New Orleans and two shows for the public. Well-known singers to perform on the show. White carpet down the aisle. The town of New Orleans gave me everything from a trousseau to furniture for the house. We had 14,000 people in the City Auditorium at two dollars a head.

"We went to court on October 17TH. My dad was my witness. My ex-husband didn't appear. I didn't know a judgment from something good to eat.

I didn't know that there was something else to be done. Louis Lyons was my attorney at that time. He failed to tell me that a judgment or something had to be read in court aloud before my divorce was granted. I said, 'You mean I'm free to marry?' He said, 'Yes, don't worry about it.' This was Friday the 17TH.

"Saturday the 18TH, Hank was on the Louisiana Hayride. Audrey had been threatening him the entire time he was in Louisiana. She would come down [from Nashville], and she said that when we married on stage that she could cause a public scene. When the preacher said, 'Does anybody know why y'all shouldn't be married?' she was gonna stand up. So this was on Saturday. Hank says, 'Well, why don't we just go get married tonight?' We had our license. 'In case she does show up, then we'll be married, and there's nothing she can do but cause a scene in public.' There were some mutual friends of mine and Hank's, Mister and Mrs. Paul Howard, visiting the Louisiana Hayride, and Hank asked them if they would go with us to find a justice of the peace. So we borrowed my brother's car because we were afraid to take Hank's car in case she was hanging around outside and filled the car full of lead. So we borrowed my brother's car, which was a 1950 Ford, and we went out in the country toward Minden, and got married. My brother never put more than a dollar's worth of gas in the car at any time, and on the way back, way out in the woods, we ran out of gas.

"So Hank got out and he started flagging a ride. Here are Mr. and Mrs. Howard, Hank and myself. Hank had on a white cowboy outfit. I had spilled my purse and make-up out on the car seat. My rouge was spilled all over the back seat, and Hank sat down in it, and his whole rear end was red from the rouge, and here he is out hitch-hiking late at night. This fellow stopped. We piled in the car, and he took us all the way home. Hank asked this fellow to spend the night with us. I said, 'You don't want to do that, not on our wedding night.' We were already stuck with his manager, Clyde Perdue, in the apartment we're renting. We had just a two-bedroom apartment.

"The next morning we went to New Orleans. The first ceremony was just about to begin when the preacher showed up to marry us and found that we were already married. He looked at our license and said, 'I can't do this.' The people were stacked in there, hanging off the rafters. Anyway, Oscar located a preacher that would do it. After the wedding, Oscar had chartered us a plane to fly us to Cuba on our honeymoon, but we were too exhausted, so we went back and spent the night in the hotel. The next day, we went back home. His manager drove us back. Then we went out on tour." (*Billie Jean Williams Berlin, deposition, December 13, 1968, re. Civil Action No. 12,181,* Billie Jean Williams Berlin vs. MGM Inc.)

The Rev. L. R. Shelton of First Baptist Church, Algiers, Louisiana, officiates.

Hank plays at his own wedding. L-R: unknown (steel guitar); Hank; Tommy Bishop; Tommy Hill

"Faron Young made the unfortunate error of introducing [Billie Jean] to Hank, who loved women. He must have loved those tits because they were tremendous. You could take any one of those and compete with a Graf Zeppelin. Plenty big. They used to get drunk down in Bossier City. I was up in Canada, and he induced me to come back. I came back to Shreveport to start over. He was living in a horrible, horrible motel. Sparsely furnished. An old kitchen table and junk all around. Every night, we had to go out and sit and drink. She would call him the damndest names. I think [Hank's] primary interest in Billie was to make Audrey jealous. Even the morning before the show at which he was married to Billie Jean on stage in New Orleans, he says, 'I know Audrey will be down to stop this.' He was hoping." *(Hank's manager Oscar Davis, interviewed by the Country Music Foundation Oral History Project, September 25, 1974)*

"Hank and Billie Jean left each other two or three times a day. I don't think he was thinking about getting back with Audrey. As far as what I knew, they would have got along okay if Hank had have stayed off the booze. He acted like he loved the woman. I also seen him beat the hell out of her. I've seen him work her over and her work him over. That's what booze will do." *(Louisiana Hayride musician Tommy Hill, September 2, 1992)*

Hank worked for the Louisiana Hayride between September and December 1952. He was back where he'd started, but this time he was the star attraction.

(top) At Hayes Record Shop, Austin, Texas, October 1952

(bottom) With a fan in Biloxi, Mississippi

(top, left) Hank introduces Billie Jean on stage during a Hayride tour

(top, right) On a Hayride tour

(bottom, left) Flanked by steel guitarist Jimmy Day (left) and Tommy Bishop (right) on a Hayride tour that touched down in Biloxi, Mississippi, on December 7, 1952

(bottom, right) On the Louisiana Hayride with Tommy Hill on guitar

In October, Hank engaged the services of a bogus physician, Horace "Toby" Marshall, who, it was later revealed, had bought his diploma from a traveling salesman. Marshall had been recommended as a therapist who specialized in the treatment of alcoholics. A former alcoholic himself, Marshall brought empathy and limitless time to Hank's problems, holding out hope of a cure. Hank had a country person's wariness of doctors but thought he'd finally found one he trusted. Marshall began treating Hank with a narcotic sedative, chloral hydrate (now known to be potentially lethal), and Hank hired him as his personal physician.

Toby Marshall

"Me and a bunch of the pickers talked about how Clyde Perdue and Toby Marshall were just in it for what they could get out of Hank 'cause he was making pretty fair money, but Hank never saw any of it. You see, if Hank took one shot of whiskey he was drunk, but he could drink a few beers, so they'd get a six-pack and allot him so many beers after he woke up until the time of the show and that kept Hank happy. Then the doctor would give him a shot so he'd lose all this beer, throw it all up, then they'd put black coffee down him, let him do the show, then give him a six pack and put him to bed. Same thing every day. I said, 'They're killing him.' The booker and the doctor. They were sons of bitches. Hank acted like he just didn't care any more. One time in Orange, Texas, we went into a bar, full of oil riggers, and Hank said, 'Okay you sons of bitches...' He had his coat pockets stuffed with money. He pulled it out, threw it on the floor. No one pocketed one bill, they just picked it up and put it on the bar. Hank said, 'The next round's on me.' He said, 'I'm playin' tonight. I 'spect to see all you sons of bitches at the show.' Damn if they weren't." *(Tommy Hill, September 2, 1992)*

Hank's last Hayride tour started in Houston, Texas, and ended in Austin on December 19.

"[My sister] Goldie Hill and I took Hank to Houston. We were going to San Antonio, and Billie Jean gave us one hundred dollars to take Hank to Houston. We had all worked the Hayride, and we left after the show 'cause Hank was working Cook's Hoedown [in Houston] on Sunday night. He just quit breathing in the car. He turned black. He had his head down between his legs, and I heard this groan. Goldie hollered at me, 'Hank can't get his breath.' He was just smothering hisself. Goldie was screaming. I stopped the car, pulled him out, and started hauling him around on my shoulders. We got to Houston about daylight Sunday. I pulled into the Rice Hotel, asked for four porters and a stretcher and got Hank up to his room. He wouldn't go to no doctor." *(Tommy Hill, interviewed March 2, 2001)*

By some accounts, Hank had a heart attack in Houston. Lillie was called and flew in.

"Hank's mother came in to San Antonio, and someone picked her up and brought her to Austin for the last show on the tour. She was there that night. It was kinda weird the way the show went....It started at eight o'clock, and now it was about nine, and Hank would usually do 30 or 45 minutes, but that night he was still singing at one o'clock. He did not quit. He put on one of the best shows I ever saw. He didn't falter a bit. He done some songs over and over. He sung everything he knew, and a bunch of gospel songs." *(Hank's supporting act, Tommy Hill, September 2, 1992)*

Hank and Lillie and his manager, Clyde Perdue, returned to Shreveport after the Austin show on Friday, December 19. They didn't stay for the Saturday night Hayride, but picked up Billie Jean and started out for Montgomery. Lillie and Billie Jean had only met once or twice, and on one of those occasions, Billie Jean had stopped Hank from giving Lillie the money for another boarding house, so Lillie's relationship with Hank's new bride was frosty at best.

"Hank Williams, the South's most remarkable and perhaps most autobiographical troubadour, is home for the holidays. With him is his new wife, the former Miss Billie Jean Jones. She's brunette, petite, and obviously more than adequate insurance for many a future Williams heart song. More than 14,000 fans attended the wedding in New Orleans in October....The high point of the show according to Hank was 'when I played "Jumbalaya" those Frenchmen roared the roof off. They went crazy.'" (Alabama Journal, *Montgomery, December 29, 1952*)

On December 28th, Hank played his last show, a private Musicians Union benefit.

"Another star of the show the musicians put on for themselves was a thin, tired-looking ex-country boy with a guitar. He got up and sang (or howled) a number of his tunes that started out to be hillbilly and ended up as pop numbers, played and sung by every band in the land. The boy who once worked here for eleven dollars a week in the Depression sung 'Jumbalaya,' 'Cold, Cold Heart,' 'You Win Again,' and 'Lovesick Blues.' There was thunderous applause as he went back to his steak. He was, of course, Hank Williams." (Alabama Journal, *Montgomery, December 30, 1952*)

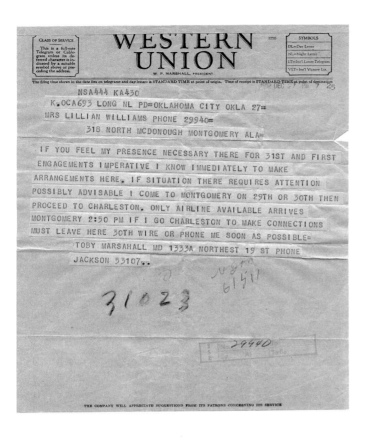

The last known photo of Hank alive taken at the Montgomery Musicians Union benefit.

"To the average modern musician, frequently called 'jazzmen,' and also the serious musician, often called 'squares' or 'longhair,' folk music or hillbilly music is not to their taste. When Hank Williams played and sang to us at the Musicians Party, December 28, all of us, including the above two groups, were there. We listened attentively as if attending a concert by Benny Goodman or hearing the cultivated voice of some operatic star. We forgot our talent, our technical skill, and musical training and truly enjoyed every note." (*Tom Hewlett, president of local AFM 479, Montgomery, Alabama, 1953*)

Bobbie Jett was still in Montgomery, but it's unknown if Hank saw her after his return. He was sick with flu for several days and was in such bad shape that there was some doubt whether he would be able to make two showdates that had been booked the previous October. The first was in Charleston, West Virginia, on New Year's Eve, and the second was a New Year's Day show in Canton, Ohio. Bad weather forced Hank to abandon plans to fly; unable to drive because of his always-agonizing back problems, he hired a student, Charles Carr, as his chauffeur. They left on December 30. Billie maintains that she originally planned to accompany him but returned to Shreveport for New Year's instead.

"He went down to the chapel at St. Jude's hospital, and he said, 'Ol' Hank needs to straighten up some things with the Man.' I said, 'Hank, what in the world is the matter with you?' He'd say, 'Every time I close my eyes, I see Jesus coming down the road.' He couldn't even sleep in bed then, the pain was so bad. When he left, he was looking at me kinda funny. I said, 'Hank, are you sick?' He said, 'Naw, babe, ol' Hank just wants to look at you one more time.'" (*Billie Jean Williams, 1991*)

Dec 28, 1952

Dear Hank,

Just received your Mother's wire that you were doing fine and felt capable of making the Charleston & Canton engagement on your own. Boy, I am tickled and pleased as I can be. and I know that if you feel good you will really put on a top-flight performance.

There is only one thing I ask, Hank, and this you morally owe to yourself, me, and your public. If you run into trouble call me. Don't for Heavens sake let the pattern run too long or get too deep before you holler. And there is nothing wrong about an old Boy asking for help when he is sick. And no matter where you are, or what the circumstances may be, I'll manage to get there. And you know I can help you.

I have talked to Vinita several times regarding your engagement here on Feb 22nd, and based on my assurance that you are doing O.K. I believe she is writing you regarding 5 or 6 more auditorium dates here for February. This is the sort of thing you need, rather than beer joints and honky-tonks, to get you back on top where you belong. I suggest you give some serious consideration to whatever she comes up with. If you are going back to the Opry you need some top-flight bookings to help things along.

The Adolphus Hotel forwarded the package containing your Honkies to me — and I re-mailed them to you yesterday.

Being the Holiday season the jug-heads around here are really getting with it. As a result I am on the run. This note is being written on a magazine on my knee while waiting for a druggist to fill some prescriptions. You'll be lucky if you can read it.

I sincerely hope your mother recovered. She was really very sick when you were at Austin and if there were not important factors involved I would have recommended Hospitalization for her for several days. She is a very wonderful, understanding, person and I both enjoyed meeting her and liked her. Sorta miss worrying about you, though, for 18-20 hrs a day several days running — But as I said above I am glad things are O.K. Your Mother said in her view that I would "hear" from you later. I certainly hope you do write me, Hank, or call, or something.

Excuse the scrawl — and good luck

Toby

Toby Marshall, M.D.
1333-A NE 19th ST
OKLA CITY, OKLA
Ph: JACKSON 53107 — home
JACKSON 8-2121 — DOCTORS BUREAU (they always know where I am)

The events of that last ride may forever remain uncertain.
The Charleston showdate was canceled because of bad weather.
Hank was in Knoxville, Tennessee, when he got word of the
cancellation. He received some injections for back pain from
at least one local physician and took a hotel room. Charles Carr
phoned the promoter, A. V. Bamford, who ordered him to resume
the journey so that Hank would be certain of appearing in Canton.
They left Knoxville at 10:45 P.M. on New Year's Eve. There was
some suspicion that Hank was dying as porters carried him to the
car, and a patrolman who stopped the car for speeding in Rutledge,
Tennessee, around 11:00 P.M. certainly thought that Hank was
already dead. Carr took on a relief driver in Bristol, Tennessee,
then proceeded north. Stopping near Oak Hill, West Virginia,
early on New Year's morning, January 1,
1953, Carr found Hank blue and lifeless.

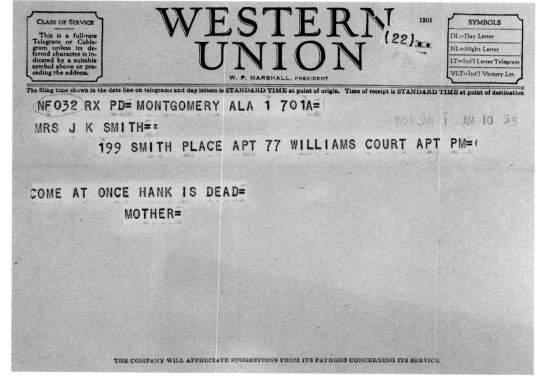

Lillie's telegram to Irene

A song fragment was found on the floor of the car.

We met we lived
and dear we loved
Then came that fatal day
The love that
felt so dear fades far
away
To night we both
are all alone and here's
all that I can say
I love you still and
always will
But that's the price
we have to
pay

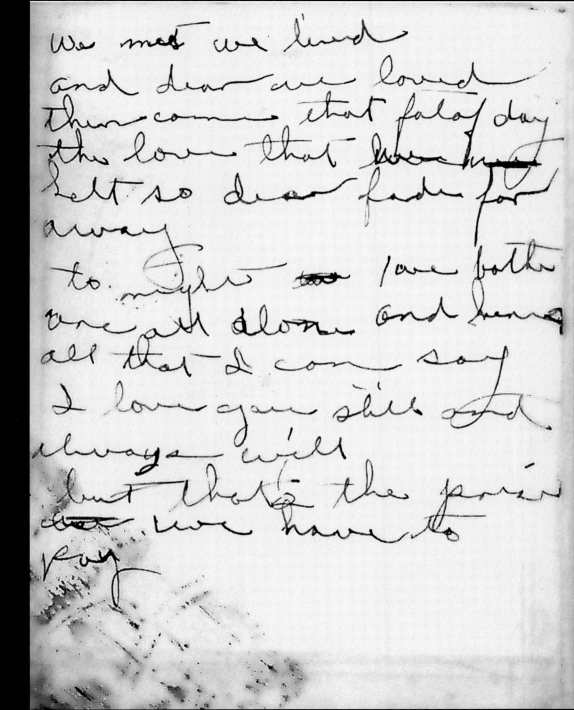

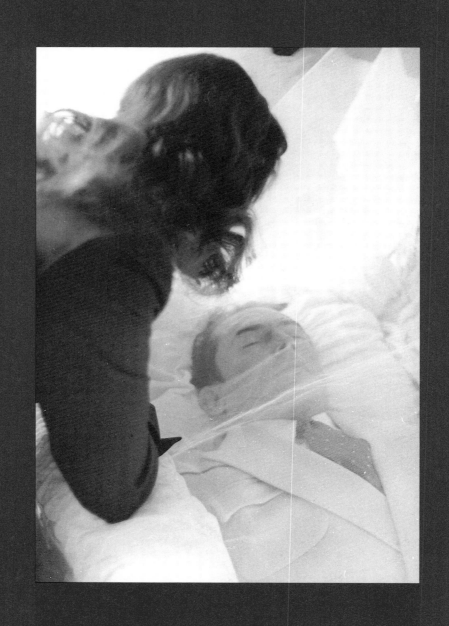

8 THE FUNERAL

"Sometime during the night, I was asleep and the telephone rang. I got up and answered. I was with my parents in their home, and the operator asked for Sergeant Jones, which was my dad. I said, 'No operator, it's for me. It's my husband. He's probably drunk.' Anyway, the operator said, 'No it's for a Sergeant Jones.' I said, 'Well, he's here, just wait a minute.' I said, 'Daddy, the call is from West Virginia, so Hank must be in trouble.' Usually, he would call my dad, if he was stopped for speeding or something. I went and laid back down, and daddy answered the phone and I heard him mumble, 'Well, where are you now?' And I just assumed he was talking to Hank, but it was the chauffeur. Hank was dead. Hank's mother chartered a plane and went up to the funeral home. By the time I got there, she had hid the car from me, taken all his possessions from his body, his billfold, his rings, everything personal, all the money that he had." *(Billie Jean Williams Berlin, deposition, December 13, 1968)*

Billie Jean bids farewell.

"My wife, Maxine, spent New Year's Eve with Audrey at the Plantation Club in Nashville. About 6:00 A.M. Maxine received a telephone call from Audrey telling her that Hank had passed away en route. After the Canton date, I returned to Nashville. There was no one in command of the funeral arrangements, so I offered to handle them. Knowing that no church could accommodate that many mourners, I made arrangements with the Montgomery Auditorium to hold the funeral there. Meanwhile, Hank was lying in state at his mother's home in Montgomery where thousands of friends and fans filed past his casket. The body was moved to the Auditorium where 30,000 more persons waited to pay their homage to Hank." *(Promoter A. V. Bamford, 1962)*

In a letter connected with one of Billie Jean's lawsuits, Hank's sister, Irene, recalled Lillie talking about Hank and Billie's last night in Montgomery. Billie had just been told that she and Hank were not legally married because her divorce from Harrison Eshliman was not final.

Audrey's mother, Artie Hardin Sheppard, with Audrey and Lillie in Hank's bedroom

"The morning Mother returned from West Virginia with Hank's body, she told me about the fight she and Billy [sic] had. Seems they [Hank and Billie] were arguing and Billie told him that she wasn't married to him and had been advised so by the judge (who later told this to the newspapers), that she was leaving the next morning, that her footlocker was packed, and he could send it to her when he got back....When [Billie] was contacted, she and her father, possibly her brother, did fly to West Virginia. Her first words on entering the funeral polar [sic] were, 'Where is my baby, if I can only kiss him, I can breathe life back into him.' This I understand she proceeded to do, became quiet [sic] hysterical and had to be removed from the room. Once she was convinced he was dead, she turned to my mother and asked where the car was. As you remember, Mother did hide the car from her and did return to Montgomery by car, and Billie did return by plane and got back the night before mother did. I welcomed Billie and her father, did everything I could to make them comfortable, and spent most of the night listening to her. The next morning when mother returned, Billie refused to speak to her. Mother went into her bedroom and sat down on the bed. Billie came out of the bedroom where she had spent the night, picked up the telephone which was on the wall in the hall and placed a long distance call to her attorney in Shreveport. Her words to him were, 'Get up here, this old gray haired bitch is trying to steal all of Hank's stuff from me.' Mother told me that if I did not get her out of the house, she would kill her.

"Mother then told me that Billie did not like the suit that had been put on Hank at the Funeral Home in West Virginia, and that she wanted me to take her to a men's shop on Dexter Avenue where Hank traded and pick out a new suit and tie. I went back to the bathroom where Billie, her father and her brother were talking as she finished putting on her make-up. I told her what my mother had told her, that I would be ready in a few minutes to go with her. Her words were, 'This is your mother's show, let her run it.' My words were, 'This is no show, it's my brother's funeral.' ... I was so mad, I could have killed her myself. I just said, 'Billie, I have tried to love you and treat you good because I figured Hank loved you or he would not have married you, but let me say something to you here and now...I will go through this funeral by your side. I will go with you to pick out the suit and tie. I realize that you think you are the meanest woman alive, but honey you have now met on [sic] much meaner than you. Now come on, we have a job to do. When it is over, don't ever cross my path again.' At this time, my mother comes into the bathroom and starts for Billie. I made her go back to her room, took Billie by the arm, very calmly walked out the front door with she and her father and brother, went to the clothing shop where she again changed her mind. Hank was buried in the suit that was picked out in the first place.

"Billie's mother arrived from Shreveport and it was decided that they would be more comfortable in a hotel. The night before the funeral, Dr. Toby Marshall showed up. Billie comes strolling in in of all things, red slacks, going from one group of people to another telling them what the ole gray haired bitch has done to her or was trying to do to her cars and possessions. Billie and Doctor Marshall got into a pretty good discussion, and he told her very frankly what he thought about her attire and her conduct." *(Irene Williams Smith, letter to attorney Robert B. Stewart, January 28, 1972)*

Braxton Schuffert's final farewell

Hank lies in state in the boarding house.

Billie Jean leaves the boarding house accompanied by her father, Sergeant J. A. Jones, and her mother, Mary Lou Jones.

Hank's body leaves the boarding house. The pallbearers include Wesley and Fred Rose.

Irene is comforted by Charles Carr, the driver.

Billie Jean en route to the City Auditorium with her parents

"There was terrific friction between Audrey, Billie Jean, and Hank's mother. There was a briefcase of songs that they were all looking for, and they found it in Billie Jean's room, and they got it while she was in the toilet and gave it to me and I put it in the trunk of my car. The following day I gave it to Fred Rose." *(A. V. Bamford, January 26, 1992)*

The squabbles during the laying-in-state presaged many years of legal battles over Hank's estate. Audrey and Lillie, who had hated each other while Hank was alive, united against Billie. From the moment Hank was buried, there was dissent over the administration of the estate and—later—renewal of the song copyrights and division of royalties.

L-R: Hank's former bassist Hillous Butrum (obscured), Ernest Tubb, Jerry Rivers, Sammy Pruett, Don Helms

Dr. Henry L. Lyons, preaching Hank's funeral

"The eeriest thing I ever had to do in my life was at Hank's funeral when the various artists sang, I had to stand up there and play with Hank's coffin right below me. I can never explain how I felt playing his songs for somebody else the way I played for him with him laying in his coffin." *(Don Helms, 1992)*

"Hank Williams, singing idol of millions of Americans, has just answered the call of the last roundup. If this world should last a thousand years, Hank shall remain dear to millions of hearts. I cannot preach the funeral of Hank Williams. It has already been preached in music and song on the radio….Since the sad message of his death was announced Thursday, the preacher of the message on the radio was Hank Williams and the congregation was the American people. His life is a real personification of what can happen in this country. Upon hearing of his death, a citizen of Montgomery was quoted as saying, 'Why, this young man, Hank, as a boy used to shine my shoes.' Hank shined that man's shoes and thousands of shoes, and even then he was singing with every snap and every pop of his shoebrush. We shall ever remember the man who climbed from the shoeshine stand to the heights of immortal glory. We thank God for our great American country which gives us the privilege to sing like we want to sing. Millions and millions never tire of the heart appeal of Hank's songs. As long as we shall have America with its freedom for individuals to succeed we will have Hank Williams to inspire us in the midst of life's hardships. Hank Williams was a great American and a great Alabamian. What was the secret of his greatness? Listen, I'll tell you what it was. He had a message. It was swelling in his bosom like a great body of water behind a great massive dam. It was a message of the heart. Deep down in the citadel of his inner being, there was desire, burden, fear, ambition, reverse after reverse, bitter disappointment, joy, success, and above all love for people. It was all there in Hank's heart. The break had to come. It did come. It came with Hank playing his guitar, singing as only a freeborn American can sing. When Hank played on his guitar, he played on the heartstrings on millions of Americans. They listened in their home, in the bus stations, in the car, in the prisons, in the office. They listened everywhere. White and colored, rich and poor, the illiterate and the educated, the young and the old. We all listened. Why? Hank had a message. It was written in the language of all the people. It was the message of the things everyone feels. Life itself. Years ago, one of America's greatest doctors said, 'If you have something that represents the genuine need of humanity, though you live in a cottage deep in the forest, mankind will beat a trail to your door.' Hank Williams had something humanity universally needs: a song with a human heartfelt message.

"My friends, before we have our benediction, I know without saying that you walk in the name of your friend and my friend Hank Williams. Please stand with your heads reverently bowed until the procession has left the auditorium, and then when we as a congregation shall leave, because we are in great number, we're in the hands of our friends, the police officers and the firemen, we're going to obey their every wish in going onward toward the cemetery."
(Dr. Henry L. Lyons)

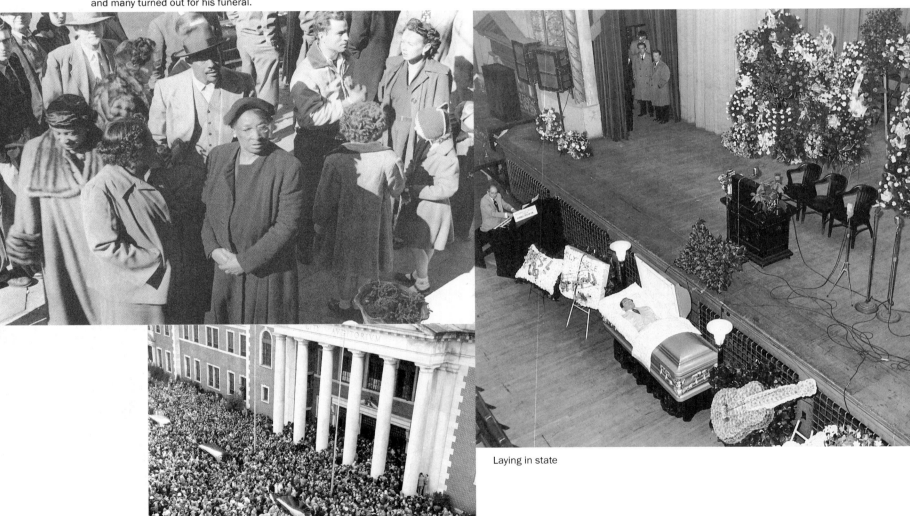

Hank had a large following among the black community,
and many turned out for his funeral.

Laying in state

The largest crowd seen in Montgomery
since the fall of the Confederacy

Myrna Fay, a friend of Hank's,
has to be led away.

The Grand Ole Opry reclaims Hank. L-R: Roy Acuff,
Red Foley, Carl Smith, Webb Pierce, Hillous Butrum

Front row, L-R: Audrey; unknown; Ernest Tubb
comforting Lillie; Lillie's fourth husband, Bill
Stone; Audrey's mother, Artie Hardin Sheppard.
Second row, L-R: unknown; unknown; Billie
Jean's brother, Sonny Jones; Capt. J. A. Jones;
Billie Jean; Mary Lou Jones; unknown
Second from back row: Ora Skipper (with
feathered hat and glasses) seated next to
Hank's cousin, Taft Skipper

Roy Acuff: "Among the friends of Hank Williams, we have the members of this colored quartet, the Southwind Singers, who will bring their message to us." Very few white citizens of Montgomery had a "colored quartet" at their funeral, but it was indicative of Hank's love of black gospel music and blues that the Southwind Singers performed.

Oakwood Cemetery

(top, right) Bill Stone and Ernest Tubb
comfort Lillie.

(right) Billie Jean with her brother,
Sonny Jones, and her mother, Mary Lou

9 AFTERMATH

January 6, 1953. Bobbie Jett gave birth to a daughter, Antha Belle Jett, who was adopted by Lillie and renamed Cathy Yvonne Stone. Readopted after Lillie's death, she was again renamed, this time Cathy Louise Deupree. Only after she came into a two-thousand-dollar bequest from Lillie on her twenty-first birthday—just three months before Bobbie Jett died—did Cathy Louise begin the pursuit of her paternity. Later, as Jett Williams, she challenged successfully for a share of Hank's estate.

Audrey and Lillie, who seemed to get along better after Hank's death, are seen here with Nashville deejay Smilin' Eddie Hill.

The Marquee

Theatre and Concert Program Publications
Oklahoma City, Oklahoma

October 5th 1952

MRS. DELBERT F. CRAVENS,
MUNICIPAL AUDITORIUM

I hereby agree to make a personal appearance for two performances (Mat & Night) in Okla City, Okla at the Municipal Auditorium under the sponsorship of Mrs Delbert F. Cravens on Sunday February 22 1953 for the total sum of $-- . I also agree to make no professional appearance in Oklahoma City for 60 days prior to February 22, 1953.

With Band 750.00

Hank Will—

—

Signature Witnessed by:

Toby Marshall

Although it was widely reported after Hank's death that he would have returned to Nashville had he lived, the only firm showdate he had lined up was at the Marquee in Oklahoma City, February 25.

POSTHUMOUS PRAISE

Fans Rush to Buy Williams' Records

20,000 Attend Williams Rites

Hillbily Singer Buried in Alabama

Step-Daughter Not Adopted:

Hank Planned To Remarry Her In February, Former Wife Says

By RICARDO BROWN and MARTHA GARRETT

Blonde, honey-voiced Audrey Williams, ex-wife of Hillbilly Star Hank Williams, today denied reports that Lycrecia, her 11-year-old daughter by a former marriage, was legally adopted by the singer

'Phony' Doctor Testifies:

Strong Sedative Prescribed For Late Hank Williams

OKLAHOMA CITY (AP)—An ex-convict and self-styled doctor who admitted to a legislative investigating committee he "never went beyond high school," testified last night he prescribed a powerful sedative and heart depressant for Hillbilly Singer

cal degrees.

Marshall is on parole from the State Penitentiary on a forgery conviction. He agreed to testify after he was jailed by Pardon and Parole Officer Campbell Leflore for refusing to cooperate the

Heart Condition Killed Hank, Coroner's Jury Says In Report

JANUARY 11, 1953

A coroner's jury decided in Oak Hill, W.Va., yesterday that the death of popular hillbilly singer Hank Williams was due to a heart condition and hemorrhaging.

The 29-year-old radio and recording star, composer of the recent song hit "Jambalaya," died in his automobile while en route from Knoxville, Tenn., to Canton, O., to fill a New Year's Day engagement.

Heart

(Continued From Page 1)

was delayed pending receipt of reports of Laboratory examinations.

Meanwhile, in Montgomery where Williams' first wife, Mrs

Hank Williams Probe Spreads Into 5 States

Effort Made To Learn If Convict Played Role In Death

From AP Reports

An Oklahoma narcotics investi-

2nd Death Laid To Fake Doctor

Strong Sedative Dose Killed Hank Williams, Phony Physician's Wife

Inquest Planned Today In Hank Williams' Death

An inquest as to the cause of death of headline hillbilly singing

Carr said Williams consulted a physician before leaving Knoxville

Fred Rose
3621 Rainbow Trail
Nashville 4, Tennessee

It is written that "AS A MAN THINKETH, SO IS HE" so I would like to tell you what I think in my heart regarding a very dear friend of mine, Hank Williams. I hope you will not think I am lost in a maze of superficial religion before you read all of what I have to say, as I think I am too practical to delve into the transcendental, beyond the realm of reason.

I believe that Hank Williams is just as much alive today as he ever was, and if you will just listen to some of the great songs he has written and recorded, plus the GOOD deeds he has done (that are just now coming to the front) I'm sure you will agree with me. Hank's life was, and is, in his great love for country music and I intend to do all in my power to keep his songs alive eternally because I believe that is the way Hank wants it to be.

I cannot spare any sympathy for death because I do not know whether it is good or bad and I don't think anyone else does either. I feel that we will all have to wait until we go through the actual experience of what is called death before we do know what it is. Therefore, I refuse to believe that Hank has migrated to a locality called Heaven, or consigned to a state of oblivion, so I intend to see, hear and enjoy the living of Hank Williams in his music.

If you feel the same as I do about the life of Hank Williams, then you will not only be preserving Hank's great love for country music, but the loved ones who are depending on him for their livelihood. No, I am not implying that you play Hank's records more than you have been but I am implying that you do not play them any less. What Hank gave to our Music Business will never die. It will live longer than you, or me.

Excuse me for being so practical about my friend's welfare, and I am,

Gratefully yours,

Fred Rose

(left) Lillie and Irene

(below) Lillie, Audrey, and Hank Jr. sifting through the letters of condolence

After Hank's death, Fred Rose released this strangely unsentimental letter, contrasting sharply with the gooey piety of MGM President Frank Walker's open letter to Hank "c/o Songwriter's Paradise." Rose made good on his promise to work Hank as if he were an active artist/songwriter. Literally hundreds of "...Sings Hank Williams" LPs would be released in the years ahead, and "those who are depending on [Hank] for their livelihood" would not be disappointed.

January 24, 1953: The last record Hank released during his lifetime, "I'll Never Get Out of This World Alive," reached number one on *Billboard*'s country charts. "Kaw-Liga"/"Your Cheatin' Heart," followed it to number one on February 21, and "Take These Chains from My Heart" became Hank's last number-one hit on June 6, 1953. With it, the supply of unissued studio recordings was almost exhausted. MGM Records and Acuff-Rose began releasing albums that mixed overdubbed song demos and live performances with studio recordings. All of them sold exceptionally well. In the 1950s and 1960s, Hank's recordings were overdubbed with "Nashville Sound" instrumentation, choruses, and strings, updating them yet again. Starting in 1985, Hank's catalog was gradually released again in its original form, using the undubbed recordings whenever they still existed.

March 8, 1953: Toby Marshall's wife died in mysterious circumstances, leading to his unmasking as a bogus physician and an enquiry into his wife's death and Hank's death. Marshall was eventually returned to jail for parole violations.

August 26, 1953: Billie Jean received $30,000 and relinquished her claim on the estate. On September 28, she married country singer Johnny Horton.

December 1, 1954: Fred Rose died in Nashville. Control of Acuff-Rose passed to his son, Wesley.

February 26, 1955: Lillie Skipper Williams, administratrix of the estate after Hank's death, died in Montgomery. Her memorabilia passed to Irene.

August 27, 1963: Grand Ole Opry manager Jim Denny died in Nashville.

January 1, 1964: Hank Jr.'s version of "Long Gone Lonesome Blues" was released. He was 14 years old. To publicize it, Audrey scheduled an appearance in Canton, Ohio, for January 1, eleven years to the day after Hank Sr. died en route.

November 4, 1964: *Your Cheatin' Heart*, an inglorious bio-pic that had been under discussion since 1953, premiered in Montgomery. Few who had known Hank recognized the character portrayed in the movie by George Hamilton IV. Audrey, as "technical adviser" and script consultant, implied that she and Hank were still married at the time of his death and that she was waiting for him backstage in Canton. In 1968, Billie Jean sued over her portrayal, then sued successfully for a share of Hank's composer royalties when they started coming up for renewal twenty-eight years after their original copyright date.

January 21, 1970: Hank's bass player Howard Watts (who doubled as comedian Cedric Rainwater) died in Florida.

September 5, 1970: Hank Jr. scored his first number-one country hit with "All for the Love of Sunshine." Nine more number-one *Billboard* country chart hits followed over the next seventeen years.

September 15, 1970: Hank's first band member, Smith "Hezzy" Adair, died in Montgomery.

October 22, 1970: Lon Williams died in south Alabama.

September 1972: Toby Marshall died in Colorado.

April 17, 1974: Bobbie Jett died in California. She had moved to California in the summer of 1953 and married John Tippins, with whom she had six children.

April 5, 1975: Hank's first manager, Oscar Davis, died in Nashville.

November 4, 1975: Audrey Williams died in Nashville. She had managed Hank Jr. until their estrangement in May 1967, and had run booking agencies and music publishing companies. She helped discover Johnny Rivers and gave several promising songwriters, Sonny Throckmorton and Mack Vickery among them, an early break.

March 17, 1988: Hank's guitarist Sammy Pruett died in Birmingham, Alabama.

January 17, 1991: Hank's cousin Marie Harvell, who lived with Hank and Irene in Georgiana, Greenville, and Montgomery, died.

November 23, 1992: Roy Acuff died in Nashville.

March 24, 1995: Irene Williams Smith died in Dallas. In 1970, she had been jailed for smuggling cocaine across the U.S.–Mexican border, and, after her release, lived in Dallas.

June 21, 1995: Bob McNett died in Montgomery, Pennsylvania.

March 4, 1996: Minnie Pearl died in Nashville.

October 4, 1996: Hank's fiddle player Jerry Rivers died in Nashville.

October 2000: Hank's cousin J. C. McNeil died in Mobile, Alabama.

(above, left) The payment to Billie Jean. Confronted with evidence that her marriage to Hank was not legal, although they had lived common-law in several states, Billie Jean accepted what she now concedes was bad advice and took a payoff.

(above, right) Clark Van Ness, who had composed "You'll Still Be in My Heart" (the melody of which was appropriated by Hank for "Cold, Cold Heart"), was paid off on January 3, 1955.

(left) Hank's former manager, Clyde Perdue, and his chauffeur on the last ride, Charles Carr, had their expenses met.

PLEASE READ YOUR CERTIFICATE Cert. No. TD 576988

MARINE DEPARTMENT

CERTIFICATE OF INSURANCE

(HOUSEHOLD GOODS FORM) O. P. No. W 400322

THE HOME INSURANCE COMPANY NEW YORK

59 MAIDEN LANE, NEW YORK 8, N. Y.

DOES INSURE Irene W. Smith - Administratix of Estate of Hiriam H. Williams
(Owner of Goods)

ADDRESS Dallas, Texas
subject to the conditions printed on the face and back hereof.

This insurance shall not cover, attach, or contribute for more than the sum of Ten Thousand Dollars & 00/100 (10, 000.00) DOLLARS, either in case of partial or total loss, or salvage charges, or any other charges or expenses, or all combined.

On Household Goods. The term "household goods" means personal effects and property used or to be used in a dwelling when a part of the equipment or supply of such dwelling; furniture, fixtures, equipment and the property of stores, offices, museums, institutions, hospitals, or other establishments when a part of the stock, equipment, or supply of such stores, offices, museums, institutions, hospitals, or other establishments; and articles, including objects of art, displays, and exhibits, which because of their unusual nature or value require specialized handling and equipment usually employed in moving household goods.

From

To

Warehouseman's Name

DEPOSITORY INSURANCE

In consideration of additional premium to be paid monthly this Certificate is extended to cover property described on deposit, incidental to transportation, not exceeding the maximum amount of insurance stated in this Certificate while contained in the premises situate at 13 West Jefferson Street and not elsewhere, from the 15 day of March 1955 until removed from storage, at which time this insurance shall immediately cease, or unless cancelled at the request of the Assured at any time upon surrender of this Certificate, or may be cancelled at any time by the Company upon giving to the Assured five (5) days' written notice of cancellation with or without tender of any excess of paid premium, which excess, if not tendered, shall be refunded on demand. Notice of cancellation mailed to the address of the Assured stated in this Certificate, or last known address, shall be a sufficient notice.

Provided this Depository Insurance is ordered by Certificate holder named herein prior to shipment to warehouse above described, transit insurance in this Certificate shall apply without further charge providing the described goods are transported on trucks and/or trailers owned or operated by the warehouseman, and provided shipping point is not in excess of 25 miles from the warehouse. If goods are delivered on trucks and/or trailers of the warehouseman within 25 miles no charge is to be made but beyond that radius a new Certificate must be issued.

Wilmer J. Savage
Warehouseman's Verification

THIS CERTIFICATE INSURES:

All physical loss or damage from any external cause (except as hereinafter excluded).

THIS CERTIFICATE DOES NOT INSURE:

(a) Accounts, bills, currency, deeds, evidences of debt, securities, money, notes, jewelry, watches, or precious stones.

(b) Loss or damage from insects, moths, vermin, ordinary wear and tear and/or gradual deterioration, inherent vice, depreciation, and/or delay.

(c) Loss or damage caused by breakage of china, glassware, statuary, bric-a-brac or similar articles of a brittle nature, unless such property is packed by the carrier or its duly authorized agent or unless such loss or damage is directly caused by fire, collision, overturn, tornado, cyclone, or windstorm, or flood.

(d) Fur or garments trimmed with fur accepted for specific fur storage.

(e) Loss or damage caused by or resulting from: (a) hostile or warlike action in time of peace or war, including action in hindering, combating or defending against an actual, impending or expected attack, (1) by any government or sovereign power (de jure or de facto), or by any authority maintaining or using military, naval or air forces; or (2) by military, naval or air forces; or (3) by an agent of any such government, power, authority or forces; (b) any weapon of war employing atomic fission or radioactive force whether in time of peace or war; (c) insurrection, rebellion, revolution, civil war, usurped power, or action taken by governmental authority in hindering, combating or defending against such an occurrence, seizure or destruction under quarantine or customs regulations, confiscation by order of any government or public authority, or risks of contraband or illegal transportation or trade.

THIS CERTIFICATE IS MADE AND ACCEPTED SUBJECT TO THE FOREGOING STIPULATIONS AND CONDITIONS AND TO THE CONDITIONS PRINTED ON THE BACK HEREOF, WHICH ARE HEREBY SPECIALLY REFERRED TO AND MADE A PART OF THIS CERTIFICATE, together with such other provisions, agreements or conditions as may be endorsed hereon or added hereto; and no officer, agent or other representative of this Company shall have power to waive or be deemed to have waived any provision or condition of this Certificate unless such waiver, if any, shall be written upon or attached hereto, nor shall any privilege or permission affecting the insurance under this Certificate exist or be claimed by the Assured unless so written or attached.

RATES PER $100. OF VALUE (Warehouseman please mark "X" in boxes applying to this Certificate)

☐ Transit under 25 miles. ☐ Transit over 25 miles but not over 200. ☐ Transit over 200 miles. ☒ Depository.

Amount $10,000.00 Premium $ 6.00 Not valid unless countersigned by a duly authorized Agent of this Company

Secretary

President

I. BERMAN COMPANY, Inc.

By L. Gilliland
Authorized Signature

March 15, 1955 19 Agent.

M. 2332B—25M Sets-3-51
Printed in U.S.A.

SEE OTHER CONTRACT CONDITIONS ON BACK OF THIS CERTIFICATE

8.	Carton	3-Albums W/36 Records 1-Scrap Book 1-Loving Cup 1-Silver Heart Award 2-Framed Letters 2-Pictures 4-Guitar Picks
9.	Carton	2 Guitars in cases - 1-Fiddle in case
10.	Carton	15 Shirts 1-Brief Case 2-Val Pacs 2- Trophies 30-Neck Ties- Assorted Letters
11.	Tie Case	17- Ties
12.	Carton	Assorted Mail
13.	Carton	Assorted Mail
14.	Leather Suitcase	Empty
15.	Leather Suitcase	Empty
16.	Recorder & Record Player	
17.	Shot Gun (in Office)	
18.	Shot Gun (In Office)	
19.	Shot Gun (In Office)	
20.	Glass Chest	
21.	Large Showcase	
22.	Saddle	
23.	Saddle Table	
24.	Picture W/Song Titles	
25.	Framed Citation	
26.	Framed Citation	

Item No.	Article
27.	Framed Citation
28.	Framed Citation
29.	Picture Frame
30.	Picture Frame
31.	Picture
32.	Picture Frame
33.	Picture Frame
34.	Picture Frame
35.	2 Pieces Glass
36.	Oil Painting
37.	Not Used
38.	Green Lounge Chair
39.	Gun Case Door
40.	Showcase Shelf
41.	Name Plate
42.	Gun Support
43.	Bundle
44.	Piece Plywood
45.	Piece Plywood
46.	Large Oil Painting

WAREHOUSE RECEIPT

NON-NEGOTIABLE

Southern Storage Warehouse Company

3 WEST JEFFERSON STREET

MONTGOMERY, ALABAMA

Lot No. 1845 Date of Issue March 15,1955, 19

Received for the account of Irene W. Smith, Administratrix of Estate of Hiriam H.Williams % Attorney Robert Stewart for storage, the goods or packages enumerated in the schedule below, upon the following terms and conditions, said goods stored in warehouse located at No.

CONDITIONS

Three months storage will be charged for any fraction of the first three months. Thereafter one month's storage will be charged for thirty days or less.

The Company when transporting acts as a private carrier only reserving the right to refuse any order for transporting and in no event is a common carrier.

This contract is accepted subject to delays or damage caused by war, insurrection, labor troubles, strikes, Acts of God or the public enemy, riots, the elements, street traffic, elevator service or other causes beyond the control of the Company.

The Company is not responsible for fragile articles injured or broken unless packed by its employees and unpacked by them at the time of delivery and in no event shall the Company be liable except for its own negligence. The Company shall not be responsible for the mechanical functions of pianos, radios, phonographs, clocks, barometers, mechanical refrigerators or other instruments or appliances whether or not such articles are packed or unpacked by the Company.

The responsibility of the Company is limited to its own negligence and no liability of any kind shall attach to this Company for any damage caused to goods by moths, other insects, vermin, rust, fire, water, fumigation or deterioration.

Unless a greater value is stated herein, the depositor declares that the value in case of loss or damage, whether arising out of the storage, transportation, packing, unpacking, fumigation, cleaning or handling of the goods, and the liability of the Company for any cause for which it may be liable, for each or any piece or package and the contents thereof, does not exceed and is limited to fifty dollars upon which declared or agreed value the rates are based, such depositor having been given the opportunity to declare a higher valuation without limitation in case of loss or damage from any cause which would make the Company liable and to pay the higher rates based thereon.

It is agreed that the address of the depositor is as given above and shall be relied upon by the Company as the address of the depositor until change of address is given in writing to the Company and acknowledged in writing by the Company, and notice of any change of address shall not be valid or binding against the Company if given or acknowledged in any other manner.

Accounts are due and payable monthly in advance. Interest will be charged on all accounts unpaid for a period of three months after they become due. All charges must be paid in cash, money order, or certified check before the delivery or transfer of goods deposited under this contract and no transfer will be recognized unless entered on the books of the Company.

Company will charge for labor and material supplied on all access to goods in the warehouse.

All claims must be made in writing within 10 days after delivery of goods. The Company shall have the right to inspect all alleged damaged articles.

This contract represents the entire agreement of the parties hereto, and is made with the agreement as to the rates and conditions as enumerated above, and applies to all services rendered by the Company for the Depositor and only an officer of the Corporation or owner or partner has power to modify the conditions of this contract, and then only in writing. The Company shall not be bound by any promise or representation at any time made, unless made in writing and signed by an officer of a Corporation or owner or partner.

All the above terms and conditions shall apply to any goods hereinafter stored for this account.

CARTAGE $
STORAGE $
LABOR $
PACKING $
$

Southern Storage
Warehouse Company
By Wilmer J. Savage (Mrs.)

ABBREVIATIONS

Bad Order	B. O.
Scratched and Marred	S. & M.
Owner's Risk	O. R.
Moth Eaten	M. E.
Contents & Condition Unknown	C. U.

SCHEDULE OF GOODS

If not correct, please notify immediately

IMPORTANT

Are your goods insured against fire? Read your policy and see that it covers the goods in the building in which they are stored.

Item No.	Article	Contents
1.	Record Case	
2.	Wardrobe	11 Suits (1 Buckskin Vest (4 Shirts (Stage Costumes 1 Jacket (1 Pair Trousers (1 Leather Jacket (Civilian 1 Overcoat, Suit & Shirt (
3.	Wardrobe	13 Civilian Suits (2 Overcoats (1 Smoking Jacket (
4.	Carton	5- Cowboy Hats
5.	Carton	6- Western Hats
6.	Carton	8 Pair Western Boots
7.	Carton	Belt & 2 Holster Sets Germany Luger Pistol & Case 45 Cal. Revolver & Holster. 45 Cal. Revolver & Holster 2- 45 Cal. Frontier Model Pistols & Holsters 3- Belts 1-Hat Strap 2-Wallets 1-Leather Shave Kit 1-Pair Gloves 1-Pair Slippers 1-Pair Oxford Shoes 1-Silver Eng. Belt 1-Crucifix 1-Chinese Figurine

ACCOUNTS PAYABLE MONTHLY

Screens, Brackets

An inventory of Hank's belongings taken just after his death.

Jett Williams, at about age 2

Lillie's shrine to Hank in Montgomery, 1953

Hank Jr. and his grandmother in
Hank's bedroom, December 1953

Funeral director Leaborne Eads drove Lillie to Nashville in Hank's car in February 1953. "Seeing it made me feel bad," Audrey wrote to Irene, "but I had the photographer come out and make some pictures."

(below right) Hank Jr. and Lillie are introduced on the stage of the Grand Ole Opry, circa 1953.

(below, left) Lillie died on February 26, 1955. Irene mourns.

(right) Lillie joins Hank in the family plot.

Hank, from his chair in heaven, provides for those left below: Lycrecia, Hank Jr., and Audrey

Wishing for you a MERRY CHRISTMAS and a GOOD YEAR

Hank Williams' House Opened To Shoppers

By MARSHA VANDE BERG

Audrey's last years were not happy ones. She became a familiar figure at industry events around Nashville, often drinking to excess. She's seen here with Jerry Lee and Linda Gail Lewis. Lawsuits and an extravagant lifestyle depleted her finances, and late in life she was forced to sell off some of her possessions in yard sales.

"I shall never forget that moment in time when I first learned with moral certainty that my daddy was Hank Williams. It was late one evening in 1984, when Keith Adkinson, then just my lawyer, called me and asked, 'Would you like to know once and for all whether or not Hank Williams was your father? Would you like to know whether he wanted you and loved you?' My heart stopped. I had known Keith Adkinson but two weeks; he had been my lawyer but one. And after over thirty years of questions, fears, hopes, and dreams, it came down to this crystallizing moment of truth.

"I always knew I was adopted, and, like all adopted children, I fantasized that my natural parents really did love me, but perhaps they had been killed in an airplane crash or a horrible car wreck. I think all adopted children go through this thought process because we don't want to face the fact that we just weren't wanted or loved enough to keep. That was the first and longest phase of my life. That was bad enough but manageable for me. It was the next phase that about did me in. This one started when I turned twenty-one, and my second adoptive mother—the one who raised me as best she could—sat me down and told me that there was a chance my father was Hank Williams. My heart stopped then, too. But she went on to say that there was no proof, nothing I could do, and everything had been decided. Against me. She said the only reason she was telling me the 'rumor' was because I had to go to the courthouse to pick up a small amount of money set aside for me from the estate of Hank's mother, Lillian. And she was fearful the press might be there and surprise me. I went; there was no press; there was a little bit of money; and there were no answers; just more questions.

"Those of you who know my story or have read my autobiography know that I grew up loving Hank Williams—a man I knew only through his music. He was a man I considered, and still consider, the greatest singer and songwriter of all time. But to have someone tell you that he *might* be your father, but you can never find out for sure, was the worst of all worlds. I tried to find out what I could, but I just couldn't bust down that wall. That all changed that fateful September night in 1984. Keith read me the most incredible document I have ever seen. It was a pre-birth custody contract, prepared by my dad's lawyer and notarized. Not only did he acknowledge that he was my father, he was taking full custody of me, sight unseen. He didn't know if I was going to be a boy or a girl; healthy or sickly. He was taking me. I was wanted. I was the daughter of Hank Williams! I literally thought my heart would stop. But I didn't cry. I thought my quest was over, but of course the saga had just begun. I got sued for making an announcement that I was the daughter of Hank Williams. Keith sued back, and it went on for years. My daddy and I almost seemed like 'third parties' to all the wrangling and feuding. And it wasn't a time for tears, it was a time to set the record straight. Which, of course, we did. The Alabama Circuit Court ruled in 1987 that I was, in fact, the daughter of Hank Williams. I didn't cry then, either. That's what they should have done, because that's who I am. Then the Alabama Supreme Court reopened my daddy's estate and awarded me half. Later, the Federal Court in New York awarded me my proportionate share of my dad's copyright renewals and publishing. And these were important achievements. But the money was secondary to setting my father's wishes straight. And it came in a distant third to finally getting some of his property. It was in 1993—almost ten years from that September night—that Keith, who was by then my husband, lawyer, and manager, went into a lawyer's office in downtown Nashville to pick up all that I would ever have that belonged to my father. I waited anxiously in the car.

"He came out beaming with pride. And he handed me my daddy's fancy performing boots, stage costumes, hat, shirt, ties, guitar, and one of his beloved pistols. I just busted out crying as I hugged my long sought-after and always loved father. That was closure for me. I cried off and on all the way back to our farm.

"That night I did something you might think silly. I put on my dad's stage suit, rolling up the legs of his pants. I put on his hat; I put on his boots. And I hugged myself. And I cried. This was as close as I would ever get, but it was closer than I ever thought I would be." (*Jett Williams*)

The first of many memorial days, this one occurred close to what would have been Hank's thirty-first birthday. L-R: Hank Snow, Ferlin Husky, Roy Acuff, Lycrecia, Hank Jr., Audrey, Ernest Tubb

"My memories of my daddy are like little snapshots. I remember knocking something over during his radio show, and this man in this gorgeous suit and white hat turned around—I can see it now. Then once when we were in the den he was lying on the couch, and I had a hammer and I was beating up on the furniture. I hit him on his head with that hammer (there was no hair on the top of his head) and I can see him laying there, on that couch, long black sideburns, curly hair, and he looked like he was seven feet tall.

"I remember being in Henry Cannon's airplane with Daddy. He couldn't sit, because of his back he had to stretch out, and I remember seeing him there like that. That's about it: the radio show, the den, and the plane.

"I know Daddy missed me. Henry Cannon told me he used to make him fly over the house when he and mother were having squabbles. He'd say on his radio show 'Bocephus, I'm coming home.'

"Not very many people knew my Daddy really well, probably not more than you could count on one hand. Jerry, Don, my mother, Minnie Pearl…He was a reluctant, hesitant star. Most of the time, he'd rather be fishing and hunting. But some people had the misconception that Daddy was rolling and lolling in sorrow, or lived with a whiskey bottle in his hand 24 hours a day, and that's not the way it was. He and his band had fun—lots of fun. They played practical jokes and they had a lot of laughs. There's so little film footage of him. People don't realize he really *moved* on stage. He was a real sharp dressed man, and his knees would gyrate—rolling around—driving the women wild, and his eyes would be dancing. When he sings 'Jambalaya' and 'Hey, Good Lookin''—the happy songs—you can tell his eyes are just twinkling. On the other hand, 'I'll Never Get Out of This World Alive' is probably better than five sessions at the shrink.

"The last two months it was all downhill. When he told Minnie 'there ain't no light' his frame of mind wasn't too good. I remember a time in my life when my frame of mind wasn't good at all—I was 26, and didn't really care if I hung around this earth or not. If you can ever get over that point—that point where a lot of entertainers, writers, and people from all walks of life reach—then you've got it made. He, unfortunately, just couldn't get over that point, at that time. If he had, who knows? Maybe he would've been happy, he definitely would've written a lot more songs, and might have had his quail farm down in Franklin…

"After he was gone I remember the Hank Williams Days. Those were some big parades down in the south for a five or six-year-old to be involved in, and they had a big influence on me. Everyone's touching you and crying, and that's when I started wondering 'Who was this man?' In the late fifties when I was going to school in the morning, there would be a busload of people in my front yard, and I would ask, 'Who are those people, Mommy?' I slowly started to realize that everyone knew him, and I needed to know him, but then I was in a bus touring myself. Listening to his songs became my real education process. You can hear anything, you can read anything, but if you sit down and listen to his albums, you'll know him, and you can make your own analysis. Just listen, you don't need anyone to explain anything to you.

"I don't think Daddy had any idea how big he was. How could he know that his music would get so big? I have my own belief that I think he knows now. I think he's seen a lot of things. He and I have winked at each other each time I get an award. I like that." *(Hank Williams, Jr.)*

SONG APPENDIX

Hank's handwriting is often difficult to read, and frequently the pencil or pen is faded, so these transcriptions are interpretive, rather than exact. We've taken liberties with them similar to those Acuff-Rose took when they typed up Hank's lyrics for their files. Some words are guesses, and there are connecting words added where they were missing. Whenever the strikeouts could be read and interpreted, we have transcribed them too. Often Hank wrote a title at the top of the page, but other songs went untitled; someone had designated lines within the songs as titles by underlining them, so we have used those lines as our titles as well. We've included dates when they are written on the pages, and date estimates when the pages of an undated lyric are sandwiched in a notebook between others which are dated. Otherwise dates are unknown. We have also indicated whether a song has been published and/or recorded before—or if this is its first publication.

I WISH I HAD A DAD   Circa late 1948. Unpublished.

I guess I'm awful lucky, my mother says I am
She says, "Why son, you have a lot" and I reply "Yes ma'am,"
I've got a knife, I've got a bike, I got a dog named Tad
I've got a lot of comic books, I've got a drawing pad
I've a Roy Rogers gun, oh, I ain't doing bad
But if I really had my wish, I'd rather have a dad

The dad I've got, you see, he comes but once a year
I ask him why he stayed away and he said "Look'a here"
And tried to take my mind away by pulling at my ear

Mom wasn't there, she never is when papa pays a call
When she came back I tried to talk but Mom said "That's all"

But there's my dog and very soon I tell it all to Tad
He asks me what it's like to have a real live dad for one whole day
And I reply gee, lots of fun
and then he wags his tail like he wishes he had one.

"Your report card must be signed by your parents" the teacher said one day,
And so I threw the card away
Cause other kids have parents, all I have is Mom
And she's alright I love her heaps, but a Mom is just a Mom,

The boys I go to school with get whippings from their Dads
I haven't had such lickin' but gee, I wish I had
Next year when he comes to see me I'll say "Papa, whale me please"
But I bet I never get him to, not even if I tease

Last time we played and romped a lot, you never saw such fun
That day he took me hunting and let me shoot the gun
But when he said "What do you want that til now you haven't had?"
I said "You was it once, could you be again? I want a full-time Dad."

I guess I'm really lucky my mother says I am,
She says "Why son, you have a lot" and I reply "Yes ma'am"
I've got a home, I've got a kite, I've got a stream line scooter,
I've got a bow and arrow and I've got a sling shot shooter
I've got a Roy Rogers gun, oh, I ain't doing bad
But if I really had my wish I'd rather have a Dad

THE OLD MAN'S LAST GOODBYE   January 26, 1947. Unpublished.

The day was slowly dying
With it a man bent and old
He called his friends to him
And to them this story he told

The years have been long and lonely
Little happiness I have known
For many years ago
God called the one that I loved home

All I had left was memories
Of a love so true and divine
But soon it will all be over
I'm leaving it all behind

Out there in the lonely churchyard
She's waited so long for me
And soon I know I'll be with her
Her dear face once more to see

Then God will welcome us together
To our new home so sweet and fair
He will straighten my old bent body
And wipe the gray from my hair

Up there we'll be young and happy
With Jesus in the sky
Where all is love and happiness
And we'll never again have to say goodbye

So don't grieve and mourn for me
~~When I go don't cry my friends~~ Where I …
I've waited so long for this day
To meet her once again

I SAW THE LIGHT   January 26, 1947. First three verses and chorus published; five additional verses and chorus (here in bold) are probably an unpublished first draft. Hank first recorded on April 21, 1947.

I wandered so aimless life filled [with] sin
I wouldn't let my dear savior in
Then Jesus came like a stranger in the night
Praise the lord, I saw the light

Chorus: I saw the light, I saw the light
No more ~~sorrow filled days and nights~~ darkness, no more night
Now I'm so happy, no sorrow in sight
Praise the lord, I saw the light

Just like a blind man I wandered alone
~~Sorrows~~ Worries and fears ~~all the day long~~ I claimed for my own
Then like the blind man that God gave back his site
Praise the lord, I saw the light

I was a fool to wander and stray
For straight is the gate and narrow is the way
Now I have traded the wrong for the right
Praise the lord, I saw the light

Once I walked in darkness
Didn't know wrong from right
Then I met my savior
(Praise the lord) I saw the light

Now my life is full of sunshine
My heart is free and light
Now I'm walking with Jesus
(Praise the lord) I saw the light

Life is so free and happy
When you travel in the light
No more sorrow and fears
Praise the lord I saw the light

Just like a blind man
That has regained his sight
Now I know my savior
Praise the lord I saw the light

Wandering so aimless in the darkness
Day was just like night
No hope for the hereafter (but
Praise the lord) I saw the light

Chorus: I saw the light, I saw the light
No more lonely days and nights
I'll meet my savior up in the sky
Praise the lord I saw the light

THIS AIN'T NO PLACE FOR ME   October 10, 1947. Unpublished.

I came to town the other day
Just to see what I could see
And I'm here to tell you now
This ain't no place for me

With all these lights and automobiles
Folks, I just don't belong
I know a mule is stubborn
But me and him can get along

A girl stopped and picked me up
In a big new shiny automobile
Then she looked at me and said
"Big boy you can take the wheel"

We started on down the road
And I told that thing to go
And the next thing I knew
We had hit a big oak tree

I sprained my arm and bent my nose
And almost broke my neck
Now folks, if I had my mule
We wouldn't have had that wreck

When I tell a mule to go
I know he's going to turn right
You can tell these cars to go
And there's no telling where you'll light

I'm going back to the country
And leave these poor crazy fools
And from now on when I ride
Friends, I'll be riding on my mule

I HOPE YOU SHED A MILLION TEARS   Unpublished.

I gave my heart and soul to you
You done me wrong so many years
Yes I hope you suffer now
I hope you shed a million tears

I hope your dreams all fade and die
And your smiles all turn to fears
May you suffer same as me
I hope you shed a million tears

THE BROKEN MARRIAGE   January 19, 1947. Unpublished.

Only two short years have passed dear
Since I heard the preacher say
"I join you two in holy wedlock
You belong to each other now from this day"

We swore then to love each other
And to never ever part
What has happened to the love we knew then
Today we are far apart

In the presence of our saviour
We said that we'd be true
But we lied my darling
Something's happened to the love we knew

Today I saw you darling
With another by your side
It hurt me so my darling
That I went home and cried

When our lives here are over
And on that judgment day
If we are still apart dear
How big a debt will we have to pay

I DIDN'T BUILD A HOUSE OF LOVE   Circa 1950. Unpublished.

Wanting to show how much I cared
~~Trying to fill your every wish~~
~~I built your beautiful home~~
I [schemed?] and built you a fine home
For this you wanted above all
~~A shrine to keep our love strong~~
A house of love to call our own

Each kiss you gave me was a lie
~~With lies you fooled my trusting heart~~
From the truth ~~you can't~~ there's no escape
I didn't build a house of love
~~But an evil mansion of hate~~ But a mansion filled with hate

~~Everybody saw but me~~
I was just a fool in love
~~I know you never did care~~
~~Not once was I in your heart~~
That I was never in your heart
You despised me at the start
You lived ~~a~~ your cruel and evil lie
~~For another owned you at the start~~

You can't find joy in my grief
You will find this out all too late
Love can't even live in a mansion
That was built with lies and hate

~~Others know your little game~~
Everyone else never bought [your] game
But to me you were sugar sweet
~~And~~ Yet hating and hoping might
Your scheme would soon be complete

PRISON OF MEMORIES   Unpublished. Recorded by Hank Jr.
(who wrote the melody) in 1967 on MGM-SE 4527.

My heart knows nothing but strife
No sunshine do I ever see
For I ~~am serving life~~ must stay all my life
In a prison of memories

My prison is not made of stone
But I ~~can~~ know I'll never ~~go~~ be free
The past is the ~~warden and guards~~ guard with the key
In my prison of memories

This world holds nothing but grief

For me life just means pain
My dungeon is deep as the sea
And know I'll never escape
From my prison of memories

~~This life holds nothing but grief~~

My life is lived in the past
Tomorrow ~~means~~ holds nothing ~~to~~ for me
Got another day to cry − regret
In my prison of memories

No key can open the door
There is no freedom for me
~~Death is the only escape~~
From my prison of memories

For years I've tried to escape

I've prayed for freedom and death
From this prison of memories

Memories of days long gone by
Sweet memories of ~~yesterday~~ that used to be
That's all the company I have
In my prison of memories

YOU KNOW THAT I KNOW   November 24, 1947. Unpublished.

You know that I know that you ain't no good
You wouldn't tell the truth if you could
Lying is a habit you practice wherever you go
You may fool the rest of this world, but you know that I know

The last time I saw you your hair was red
But today I see you've got blond hair on your head
You say you've got you an old man with plenty of dough
Baby you may fool him, but you know that I know

So baby when you pass me, don't give me the run around
'Cause if you'll remember, I'm the guy that brought you to town
To some folks [gals] you may be Mrs. so and so
But don't turn your nose up at me 'cause you know that I know

You told some of my friends that you turned me down
But I wouldn't have you if you were the last gal in town
If I had wanted you I could have got you long ago
You may fool the rest of this world, but you know that I know

THAT LAST LONG RIDE   September 18, 1948. Unpublished.

I ~~was~~ stood beside a deep cold grave
One dark and rainy day
And watched so helpless as they laid
My own dear darling away

I cried and prayed to God above
Not to take her from my side
But today I saw her take
That last long lonesome ride

I can't go on, no use to try
I wish that I could die
I am dead and yet I live
Oh God what misery

I saw the heavens all turn black
I heard the winds they cried
They seemed to whisper in my ear
She's taking that last long ride

HOMESICK   February 8, 1951. Published. Recorded by Hank Jr.
(who wrote the melody) in 1969 on MGM-SE 4621.

Homesick and lonely, worried and blue
Wanta see the baby and the baby's mama too
So tired of roaming 'bout to lose my mind
Homesick and lonesome for that gal of mine

Mean old trouble is all that I've known
I'm missing my honey boy I'm going home
If she'll just let me tarry when I come dragging in
You couldn't take a shotgun and run me off again

This old boy's got missing in his soul
This old world is too big and too cold
I'm riding that freight train when she comes down the track
And next time you see me leaving I'll be flat on my back

I never knew a body could feel so low
I keep asking myself "why did you ever go"
I'm heading home and there I'm gonna park
And if she wants it that way I'm gonna learn how to bark

HEART FILLED WITH HATE   October 9, 1951. Unpublished.

Typed Lyric

SEARCHING IN VAIN   January 17, 1951. Unpublished.

I walk the lonely streets of life day after day
Hoping and praying that you will pass my way
Longing for just a glimpse of your face again
Walking the road of life and searching in vain

Searching for a treasure that I know's forever gone
Still I walk this lonely road from twilight till dawn
Like a dove up in the blue that has lost his mate
I know I'll never find you but still I search and wait

The flowers she planted when love was true have withered now and died
The house we planned is dark and cold without her love inside
All the joys of life are gone there's nothing left but pain
As I walk the lonely road of life and search but all in vain

Sometimes I stop and tell myself there's no use to pretend
No matter how long the road, somewhere there's an end
Then I'll hear the whistle blow of a lonesome train
And my journey starts anew searching but in vain

MANSION FOR YOUR SOUL   Circa 1951. Unpublished.

If you chose the road of sin my brother
You will have to pay the toll
You may have a mansion for your body
But do you have a ~~home~~ mansion for your soul

Oh the good book says to love your brother
Help him out when he gets in a hole
Then when you leave this world here behind you
You'll find a ~~home~~ mansion for your soul

You may have a castle lined with marble
With walls made out of solid gold
But if God don't live inside your castle
You'll still need a mansion for your soul

In my father's house there's many mansions
Many times you've heard the story told
But if you never learn to love your saviour
You'll never find a mansion for your soul

When the Master's book of life is opened
And the angels start to call the roll
If you've lived according to His teachings
You'll be given a mansion for your soul

TOMORROW MAY NOT COME   Circa April 1948. Unpublished.

~~A GRAY HAIRED LADY~~

~~An old grey haired mother lay dying~~
~~She called for her only son~~
~~She said son don't wait 'til tomorrow to~~

~~Straighten up with Jesus~~
~~For tomorrow may not come~~

Dear friends don't wait 'til tomorrow
To pay for deeds you have done
Get right today with your saviour
For tomorrow may not come

In ~~this~~ a sinful world we're living
From God the people all have run
And God may make today the payday
And tomorrow may not come

In this selfish quest for power
The world forgot the holy one
They have no love for their neighbor
And tomorrow may not come

God so loved ~~these wicked people mortals~~ the wicked world
That He gave His only son
~~But this world will pay for it in full~~
But some times coming a payday
And tomorrow may not come

People call not for their saviour
Fathers kill their only sons
Daughters stand and curse their mothers
Friends tomorrow may not come

How can this world keep on standing
After all the things its people's done
Meet God today and not tomorrow
For tomorrow may not come

God so loved this wicked world
That He gave His only son
But this world's forgotten the gift...

IT WORKS ONE WAY OR THE OTHER   Unpublished.

If your mama's cross and she won't treat you right
Beat her every morning and love her every night
Then she'll do right, like a good gal ought to do
She'll quit her nagging, and making you blue

If your family life ain't what it ought to be
Then all you gotta do ~~follow this recipe~~ is take this tip from me
Then ~~you'll~~ around your house you'll see a change
Things run smooth and honey will be your name

If she fusses about every ~~thing you do~~ little thing you do
Always getting angry and sassy and just won't do
Show her who's boss, use a strong hand
Then she'll harness that temper, and bid your command

Now I tried this out and it worked just fine
I've got no more troubles, ~~I'm a single man~~ nor would mind
'Cause my old gal has done left me way behind
It works one way or the other every time

YOU HAVE GROWN TO BE A STRANGER TO ME
January 8, 1951. Unpublished.
(Lyrics in bold are not reproduced in the book.)

Where is the love that we once knew
That was so true and divine
Where are the words we used to speak
That were so soft and kind
Where are the kisses you used to give
So eager and so free
Darling you have grown to be a stranger to me

Where is the fun we used to have
Just walking hand and hand
Where are the thrills we used to get
Just dancing to a band
Where are the stars that were in your eyes
That I used to see
Darling you have grown to be a stranger to me

Where are the rides we used to take
It seems a million years ago
What has happened to our love
Tell me darling if you know
Where are the ~~midnight~~ strolls we used to take
Down by the rolling sea
Darling you have grown to be a stranger to me

Where are the plans we used to make
Darling you and I
Where are the dreams we used to dream
Have they passed us by
What's happened to all the fun and joys
Sweetheart we used to see
Before you grew to be a stranger to me

THE HEAVENS ARE LONELY TOO   February 19, 1947. Unpublished.

The night is cold and dreary
Darling just like your love
Vows you made were lies dear
And I'm blue as the heavens above

I can hear the rain a falling
It sounds so lonesome and blue
Everything around me looks so dreary
It seems the heavens are lonely too

Black clouds have covered up the moon
The stars refuse to shine
There's no sunshine left in my life
Since you left me here behind

OH MAMA COME HOME   Circa February 1947. Unpublished.
(Lyrics in bold are not reproduced in the book.)

I woke up this morning
I looked all around
It was then that I realized
That you had left this town
Oh Mama come, ~~oh mama~~ home
Oh Mama come home
Oh Mama come home your daddy is all alone

There's no one here now
To warm my bed at night
All my days are long and sad
And filled with trouble and strife
Oh Mama come home, oh mama come home,
Oh Mama come home your daddy is all alone

Your Daddy's getting worried
So blue I can't see
Cooking for these younguns
Is slowly killing me
Oh Mama come home, Oh Mama come home
Mama come home, your Daddy's all alone

Baby I'm so lonely
And nothing's going right
Blues they hang around me
Both day and night
Oh Mama come home, Oh Mama come home
Mama come home, your Daddy's all alone

YOU'VE BEEN LONESOME TOO   November 22, 1950. Unpublished.

If your heart has known such pain, until for death it's cried
Only to have the Lord refuse, then you've been near my side
If in your heart somehow you know you'll fail, what e'er you do
Then you have walked a road of pain, yes, you've been lonesome too

If you have had each joy of life destroyed and cast away
Then watch a heart that once knew love grow sadder day by day
If your soul's wilted like a rose, that never feels the dew
You're traveling on the street of grief, yes, you've been lonesome too

If for your wasted wicked life, your soul cries out in shame
And you could live it all again, it would never be the same
If you've cried "God, Please bless the one to whom I was untrue"
You've lived a life of regret, yes, you've been lonesome too

If when the stars light up the skies it seems you can't go on
Then out of a vision your darling appears, you speak but the image is gone
If though the tears cover your cheeks, there can be no other for you
You can't ever hide from fate, yes, you've been lonesome too

COLD, COLD HEART   November 23, 1950. Unpublished. Hank first recorded on December 21, 1950.

I try so hard my dear to show that you're my every dream
Yet you're afraid each thing I do is just some evil scheme
In anger unkind words are said that make the teardrops start
Why can't I free your tortured mind and melt your cold cold heart

Another ~~dear~~ love before my time made your heart sad and blue
And so my ~~poor~~ heart's paying now for things it didn't do
Memories of ~~the~~ your lonesome past keep us so far apart
Why can't I free your tortured mind and meet your cold cold heart

~~Words can't explain~~ You'll never know how much it hurts to sit and
      watch you cry
~~Knowing~~ I know you need and want my love, ~~but yet too scared~~ to try
You can't run and hide from life to try it just ain't smart
Why can't I free your ~~tortured mind and meet~~ your cold cold heart

THE DRUNKARD'S DREAM   November 24, 1947. Unpublished.

I dreamed that my dear mother so sweet
With her last breath was praying for me
"Dear God please save my precious boy
Fill his heart with heaven's joy

Dear God, please show him right from wrong
I can't help him now for I must go home
O Lord, I've failed but you know I tried"
With a tear on her cheek, my mother died

My daddy was there holding her hand
When death's angel took her to that great land
He looked so alone and helpless there
With Mother's last words ringing in his ear

Then I awoke from my drunken dream
The world had turned dark it seemed
And then in my wicked heart I knew
That all of my drunken dream was true.

I hurried to my mother's side
With burning tears in my eyes
My dad was weeping by her bed
Because my mother dear was dead

Dear God up there in heaven fair
Please hear this sinful drunkard's prayer
Tell Mother dear I see the way
And that I'll meet her some glad day

THE SERMON ON THE MOUNTAIN   January 8, 1951. Unpublished.

A man ~~stood~~ sat on a mountain side
~~He was a~~ A carpenter by trade
Teaching his disciples
~~As~~ While they knelt and prayed
He blessed the poor and simple
And brought the mourners joy
~~To heal the lame the blind the dumb~~
~~He came not to destroy~~
He came to heal the blind and lame
He came not to destroy

When [stricken?] by his enemies
He turned the other cheek
He brought the strength of spirit
To mortals who were weak
He told us of false prophets
Who wore a sheep's disguise
He wanted us not to trust them
Or listen to their lies

The sermon on the mountainside
We'll live eternally
And lead us to the kingdom
That He promised you and me
So take the straight and narrow
And find the open fount
Make up your mind to live by
The sermon on the mount

I THANK MY GOD FOR YOU   October 11, 1951. Unpublished.

When this cruel world has been unkind
And left me sad and blue
It's then I kneel in [humble] prayer
And I thank my God for you

You always meet with open arms
To understand each thing I do
And lend your hand when I am down
I thank my God for you

The understanding in your eyes
And love so kind and true
Make me the richest man on earth
And I thank my God for you

I pray to God to give me strength
So my prayers won't be too few
For you're my dream, my love, my life
I thank my God for you

WHAT CAN A HEART DO   Circa 1951. Unpublished.

What can a heart say
That's broken and blue
No one to cry to
So what can it do
No one to love now
No use to try
What can a heart do
Just pray to die

FOR ME THERE IS NO PLACE   January 8, 1951. Published,
except for last stanza. Recorded by Hank Jr. (who wrote the melody)
in 1969 on MGM-SE 4621.

You have always wanted dear
The finest things in life
~~And~~ So that your dreams could all come true

I've saved with all my might
The plans I made for you and me
Have all gone to waste
For in the world you live in now
For me there is no place

Gone is the sweet and simple girl
That I have loved so long
And in her place a stranger lives
Who wants a dream world, not a home
The hate that shows within your eyes
Has ~~smashed~~ broke my heart inside
Wealth has killed your love for me
And driven you from my side

With the sunrise I'll be gone
And then my darling you'll be free
Free to live the life you want
With no interruptions from me
For I am just a simple boy
Who didn't keep up with pace
And in the world you live in now
For me there is no place

I'M SO TIRED OF IT ALL   June 29, 1947.
Published in a slightly different form than this unpublished
(handwritten) version. Hank first recorded circa 1947.

All my life I've been so lonesome
If happiness came I missed the call
All my dreams have died and vanished
And now I'm so tired of it all

In life and love I've been a failure
Too many tears through it all
Too many broken vows and promises
And now I'm so tired of it all

Everything I've ever loved I lost it
Too many times I've watched my castles fall
My life is ~~filled~~ full of regretting
And now I'm so tired of it all

From this world I'll soon be going
No one will miss me after all
Up there I pray I'll find contentment
For now I'm so tired of it all

WHEN YOU BROKE YOUR VOW   Unpublished.

Friends say that I'll forget you
But I don't know how
You broke my heart
When you broke your vow

When the world learns again how to pray
Peace and goodwill will come back to stay
They'll sing a happy song
And everyone will get along
When the world learns again how to pray

~~Today~~ The day has been long and dreary
There's nothing but sorrow ~~?~~ now
You broke my heart
When you broke your vow

You promised to love me forever
But you lied to me somehow
You broke my heart
When you broke your vow

~~I know I'll never forget you~~
~~You'll always live in my heart~~
~~When you broke your promise~~
You broke your promise darling
And I'm so lonely now
You broke my heart
When you broke your vow

WHY DID MOMMY SAY GOODBYE   Circa February 1947. Unpublished.

One night by the fireside, sat a man and his little son
He was telling the boy stories, trying to show a little fun
But the little boy was lonely, there were tears in his eyes
Then he asked his daddy, "Why did Mommy say goodbye?"

In the man's face you could see sorrow, his heart was breaking inside
And it took the help of God, to keep the tears from his eyes
How could he tell his baby, what his mother had done
How she had forsaken them, so she could have her fun

He thought if I tell him, will it be a mistake
Or should I lie to him, and in his mother let him keep the faith
For a moment he thought it over, and this is what he said
"We'll meet Mother in heaven someday, son, your mother is dead"

That night when the child was sleeping, his Daddy said a prayer
Dear God did I do right, or was I unfair
He's so young and helpless, but he is her son
But I'd rather die today, than for him to know what she has done

HONKEY TONKIN' MAMA   June 29, 1947. Unpublished.

Listen to me little gal
You better quit your fooling around
Your daddy's getting tired
Of the way you're running around
Honkey tonkin' honkey tonkin' mama

I took you out of a honkey tonk
And gave you a home
But every time I turn my back
You are out and gone
Honkey tonkin' honkey tonkin' mama

You look so innocent
When I look into your eyes
But every time you open your mouth
I know you're gonna lie
Honkey tonkin' honkey tonkin' mama

Your baby face and big blue eyes
Made me believe in you
But hang around a honkey tonk
Is all you want to do
Honkey tonkin' honkey tonkin' mama

You sleep all day and prowl all night
You're just like an owl
Out smooching with another guy
You're a two-timing gal
Honkey tonkin' honkey tonkin' mama

You said you loved me
By all the stars above
But baby honkey tonkin'
Done got in your blood
Honkey tonkin' honkey tonkin' mama

YOU'LL NEVER AGAIN BE MINE   April 21, 1952. Unpublished.

I'm living with days that forever are gone
And a heart that does nothing but pine
To love and to want you I know is wrong
When I can never again call you mine

To worship you darling the way that I do
I know is just wasting my time
Yet my foolish heart cries each day for you
Though I can never again call you mine

I tell my poor heart to live and forget
And someday a new love it will find
But each day it lives is filled with regret
'Cause I can never again call you mine

My lonely heart holds no hatred or blame

THE DRIFTWOOD BLUES   Unpublished.
(This lyric, scrawled on both sides of an envelope, is particularly
difficult to read, so this is merely an attempt to interpret.)

Let the tide come in
And drift me away from here
For the long tall Blond has got me down again

So I have got the driftwood blues
So please come on tide and
Drift me away from here

Oh that Blond of mine has done
But her [?] ~~doesn't~~ [matter or water]
I can't go home no more just
Come on in and drift me away from here

YESTERDAY MY DREAMS ALL DIED   Unpublished.

~~Like a star that falls from heaven~~
~~My eyes can never be dried~~

Like a ~~lonely~~ dove lost in the heavens
My sorrows more than I can hide
In the ~~game of life?~~ game I've been a loser
Yesterday my dreams all died

Life sometimes can be so bitter
~~When your soul has died inside~~
No matter how hard you tried
~~Up there will I find contentment~~
Will death be sweet beyond the river
Yesterday my dreams all died

Like a ship ~~out~~ lost on the ocean
Whose only captain is the tide
Through this weary world I'm drifting
Yesterday my dreams all died

I pray you'll never know this sorrow
May happiness walk by your side
I've loved and lost, for me it's over
Yesterday my dreams all died

THEN CAME THAT FATAL DAY   Circa December 31, 1952. Unpublished.
Found on the floor of the car where Hank died. See page 173.

CREDITS

Photos courtesy of Marty Stuart: 6, 7, 20, 22 (all), 23, 25, 28, 30, 31 (all), 32, 33, 36, 38 (all), 39 (letter), 40 (letter), 41 (all), 42 (all), 43 (all), 44, 47 (top), 48, 49, 51 (all), 56-57 (all), 58 (all), 59 (all), 61, 62, 65, 66, 68, 71 (all), 72 (all), 74, 77 (all), 80 (top r, bottom), 81, 82 (all), 83 (top l and r, bottom r), 87, 90 (all), 91, 92, 94, 96 (bottom all), 100 (bottom four), 101 (all except bottom r, bottom c), 104 (top photo), 105 (all), 106, 108 (r), 110 (bottom two), 111 (top two, r, second from r), 112 (l, bottom r), 113 (top c, bottom c), 114 (top, c, l), 115 (all), 116 (r), 117 (all), 118, 119, 122 (top l, bottom), 126, 129 (lyrics), 130 (c, bottom), 131 (all), 132 (all), 133 (top r), 136, 145, 150 (program), 151 (all), 155 (lyric), 160 (receipt), 164 (bottom), 165 (all), 166 (bottom l), 167 (lyric), 169 (telegram), 170–171 (letter), 174, 175, 176, 177 (bottom), 178 (all), 179 (all), 180 (all), 182 (all), 183 (all), 184 (all), 185 (all), 186, 189 (all), 194 (l, top r, bottom r), 195 (all), 196 (all), 197 (top l, bottom l), 199 (all), 201, 208; Photos courtesy of Hank Williams Jr.: 24, 26, 34, 35, 37 (top), 47 (bottom) 52 (ad), 53 (article), 54, 55 (all except left), 80 (l), 83 (bottom l), 85 (bottom), 86 (article), 88, 89 (article), 96 (top), 97, 98 (all), 99, 100 (top), 101 (bottom r), 102 (all), 103 (all), 104 (bottom), 108 (l), 110 (top two), 112 (top c, top r), 113 (top l, bottom r), 122 (top r), 124, 133 (top l, bottom r), 146 (l), 151 (letter), 152 (letter), 153 (letter), 169, 172 (telegram), 173 (lyric), 177 (top), 188 (headlines), 197 (r, article); Lyrics courtesy of Acuff-Rose Music Inc.: 8, 29, 50, 60, 64, 69, 70, 73, 75, 76, 95, 109, 118, 119, 120, 123, 125, 126, 127, 128, 135, 137, 139, 142, 143, 144, 146 (top, bottom r), 147, 150; Photos courtesy of Jett Williams: 21, 101 (bottom c), 107 (all), 111 (bottom l), 113 (bottom l), 114 (bottom r), 116 (l, c), 135, 141, 149 (all), 154 (all), 166 (bottom r), 187, 194 (top c); Photos courtesy of Colin Escott: 45, 53 (top r), 67, 84, 104 (contract), 106 (contract), 130 (top), 138, 157, 158 (all), 159, 162, 164 (top r, top l), 188 (letter); Documents courtesy of Big Bill Lister / Colin Escott: 110 (article), 111 (ad), 133 (program); Photos courtesy of Don Daily: 78-79 (all); Photos courtesy of Glenn Sutton: 19, 63 (script), 126 (script); Photos courtesy of Daily Oklahoman / Colin Escott: 167 (top); Photos courtesy of David Dennard/Dragon Street Records: Page 113 (top r); Photos courtesy of George Merritt: 27, 93, 134 (session sheet), 160 (top); Photos courtesy of Jurgen Koop: page 166 (top r, top l); Article courtesy of Bill MacEwen: 134; Photo courtesy of Pee Wee Moultrie: 37 (bottom); Photo courtesy of Bill Whatley: 161; Photo courtesy of Pete Howard, photo taken by Neal Hamilton/Rock and Roll Hall of Fame and Museum: 156